D1431004

TYPE DESIGNS

THEIR HISTORY AND DEVELOPMENT

TYPE DESIGNS

THEIR HISTORY AND DEVELOPMENT

A. F. JOHNSON

SECOND EDITION

GRAFTON & CO

COPTIC HOUSE · LONDON WC1

1959

First edition, 1934

Made and Printed in Great Britain
by Jarrold and Sons Limited Norwich

Contents

Preface

IN PREPARING A NEW EDITION of this book I have made no attempt to enlarge the work by the addition of further chapters, but have tried merely to bring it up to date. As in the first edition I have to thank the editors of *The Library* for the loan of blocks originally made for my articles in that periodical. I have also to thank Messrs. Faber & Faber for allowing me to use some illustrations which first appeared in their new edition of T. B. Reed's *Old English Letter Foundries*, 1952. The illustrations taken from Reed are nos. 2, 6, 13, 38, 40, 42 and 43.

A. F. J.

List of Illustrations

Introduction

AS AN INTRODUCTION to the history of type forms, something may be said in outline of the story of the invention of printing. Printing from movable type was known in China long before the invention in Europe, but there seems no reason to suppose that any specimens of Chinese printing can have reached the West and we may feel confident that the European invention was new and entirely independent.[1] Works of reference frequently assert that printing was invented by Johann Gutenberg of Mainz about 1450, as though this were a definite fact, but the whole story is wrapped in obscurity, and is built up from a small number of scraps of evidence. There is no single printed book or printed fragment which bears Gutenberg's name, but there have survived several legal documents bearing on the question, and there are, moreover, the statements of contemporaries attributing the invention to Gutenberg. For example, Ulrich Gering and his partners, who brought the new art to Paris, in one of their colophons distinctly refer to Gutenberg as the inventor. The only substantial book produced by this first Mainz press was a Latin Bible, variously known as the Gutenberg Bible, the 42-line Bible, from the number of lines to a page, and the Mazarine Bible. The last name is derived from a copy which belonged to Cardinal Mazarin. Another copy in the Bibliothèque Nationale bears the signature of a rubricator from which we know that he finished his task in August 1456. In November 1455, Johann Fust of Mainz brought an action against Gutenberg for the recovery of money lent for the printing of this

[1] See T. F. Carter, *The Invention of Printing in China*, New York, 1931.

Bible and other works. We do not know whether the Bible was finished by that date, although it must have been finished soon afterwards, nor do we know the result of the action. Apparently Gutenberg lost the case, because the type of the Bible remained in the possession of Fust and Peter Schöffer, the third man in the partnership. One school argues that the Bible is Schöffer's work, basing their argument on evidence which exists that the work was rapidly printed and was probably produced after the split with Gutenberg. The case for Schöffer is not widely accepted, but the claim is another illustration of the obscurity surrounding Gutenberg's career. However, this Bible is not only the first printed book but is one of the finest books ever produced, a fact which is hardly flattering to the efforts of the typographers of five subsequent centuries.[1]

The only serious rival claimant to Gutenberg is one Laurents Coster of Haarlem. In the book known as the *Cologne Chronicle*, printed in 1499, there appears an account of the invention derived from Ulrich Zell, the first printer at Cologne, who came from Mainz. Zell states that Gutenberg was the inventor, but that he was acquainted with a "Vorbildung" in the Donatuses produced in Holland. The exact meaning of "Vorbildung" in this passage is doubtful. English textbooks have translated it as "Prefiguration", an equally vague term. There are in existence a number of fragments of early Dutch printing of a primitive appearance, which include Donatuses, that is, the school Latin grammars of the Middle Ages. The legend which attributes these fragments to Coster dates from a century later, and is full of impossibilities. Whether Coster was their printer or not is comparatively unimportant. They may be conveniently labelled "Costeriana". They exist and have to be accounted for. The controversy about these Costeriana has been long, voluminous, unnecessarily bitter through nationalist rivalry, and is still unsettled. The latest scholar to tackle the problem is Dr. G. Zedler.[2] In a massive volume, highly technical and very difficult reading, Zedler accepts the

[1] See A. Ruppel, *Johannes Gutenberg*, Berlin, 1939.
[2] *Von Coster zu Gutenberg*, Leipzig, 1921.

Costeriana as the Vorbildung of Ulrich Zell, and attempts to show how they were produced and to date them. He considers that the type was made by a process of casting in sand. No layman can really pronounce a verdict on this very technical subject. Zedler's thesis may be right, or it may not, but at least we can accept the general conclusion that the types of the Costeriana were produced by a method which proved in the end to be impracticable. They did not solve the problem of casting satisfactory type in large quantities as a commercial proposition. As to their dates Zedler's case is weak. His reconstruction of the time-table of Coster's press, in which he carries back the earliest fragments to a date before the appearance of anything at Mainz, is forced. We do not know yet as a fact that the Costeriana are earlier than Gutenberg. We have not the material to settle the question, and unless fresh documents are discovered the controversy will remain unsettled.

On the other hand, types were produced at Mainz by a method which proved to be practicable, and this method continued to be followed with very little change down to the nineteenth century. The first step is the preparation of punches; letters are engraved on the ends of punches of hard metal, a very difficult and lengthy task. The punch is struck into a piece of copper, known as a matrix or strike; the matrix, after justification, is then placed in an adjustable hand-casting machine or mould. When this machine is closed or adjusted the matrix is at the bottom of a crevice and into this crevice molten lead, or some alloy containing lead, is poured. This lead, when taken from the mould, is the type, having in relief on one end the letter derived from the impression in the matrix. This hand-casting machine was the essence of Gutenberg's invention and the discovery which made possible the book printed from movable types.

Gutenberg did not discover the means of taking an impression, he was not the first man to construct a press nor the first to engrave letters on steel, to be used as a punch. All these mechanical arts and also the art of casting were known long before his day. Still less did he or any other early printer introduce any innovation in the design of letters. On the contrary, he copied the contemporary letter formation as known in the manuscript book, and in fact gave himself endless trouble in order to make his copy as exact as possible. Dr. Paul Schwenke's[1] examination of the type of the Gutenberg Bible has revealed the number of extra sorts which were cut in order that a page of his book might be mistaken for a page written by a calligrapher. The incunable period in the history of the book, which we arbitrarily close with the year 1500, may be defined as the period in which traces of the hand-written book are still to be found. The models which the first typographers had before them were manuscripts and the dignity of the work they produced is due to the high standard of beauty maintained by the models they were following. The handsome and imposing pages of the best incunables approach the even finer pages of the best manuscripts.

[1] *Johann Gutenberg's Zweiundvierzigzeilige Bibel*, Leipzig, 1923.

CHAPTER I

Gothic Types

THE HISTORY OF the design of types is a continuation of the history of letter formation. It was not until the printed book had developed into something altogether distinct from the manuscript that the designers of type became arbiters of taste in such matters. In the sixteenth century Garamond could introduce forms which became traditional, but in 1460 this was the function of the calligraphers. It is not proposed here to trace the history of European letters from the roman alphabet through the Caroline minuscules down to the hands in use in the fifteenth century. It will be enough to point out that all the European hands are descended from the same source, the script of the Roman Empire, and that although national and local characteristics are to be found, yet the German hands of *c.* 1450 can be paralleled in Italy. These hands are known to us as gothic, a name used first in derision by Italian humanists of the Renaissance, for instance Vasari, but in fact have nothing to do with the Goths. They might more fittingly be described as medieval, for they are essentially the hands of the Middle Ages, as distinguished from the humanistic hands of the Renaissance. Early examples of the most formal of the gothic hands, the upright and angular Textura or "Lettre de forme", are found in manuscripts written at the Benedictine Monastery of Monte Cassino in southern Italy. North of the Alps this formal letter became the standard for the Bibles and service books prepared for the use of the Church. For scholastic and theological texts a less formal and rounded letter was used, for which there appears to have been no particular group name, and thirdly, for work in the vernacular, a still less formal and cursive hand known as Bastarda.

The early printers found it necessary to cut three styles of types corresponding to these three groups of books—the liturgical, the scholastic, and the vernacular. Although the types found in incunables, especially in German incunables, are of very great variety, they can nevertheless be classified according to these three groups, in a descending order of formality.

Group A. The types cut by "Coster" and all the earliest types cut by Gutenberg belong to this first group of the formal gothic hand. This is an upright and angular letter characterised by an almost entire absence of curves. It may be described as drawn rather than written (see fig. 1). The different hands are arrived at by entirely dissimilar processes of penmanship. A scribe who makes a formal gothic h follows a very different process from one writing a current h, and uses a different kind of pen. Ascenders and descenders are short and end in points known as "feet". From the point of view legibility all the letters are not sufficiently differentiated, for example, the n is merely two i's, and the m three i's, placed in contact, so that a combination such as *imn* is obscure. But legibility was not the chief aim of the medieval scribe. This formal script with its tall letters, black face, and short ascenders and descenders enabled him to produce a closely packed page with a large proportion of black to white, which had the appearance of a woven texture. The handbooks of palaeography show that the name, Textus goes back at least to the twelfth century (cf. Wattenbach, *Das Schriftwesen im Mittelalter*, 3rd edition, 1896, p. 297). The very interesting advertisement of an early fifteenth-century calligrapher, one Johann vander Hagen,[1] of Bodenwerder on the Weser, described by Wattenbach, shows a "Textus quadratus", a "Textus semiquadratus", and a "Textus sine pedibus", that is, without the pointed or diamond-shaped feet. The French call the letter "lettre de forme", and the name is used in inventories of the

[1] Reproduced in *The Library*, March 1929.

We may call this group rigid, because, given the formality of the design, there could be little scope for variation. There were variations in the matter of pointedness and narrowness and in the construction of the feet. The plates in Mr. Morison's *German Incunabula in the British Museum* give us a conspectus of the extent to which Texturs could differ. Contrast, for instance, the condensed letters of Michael Wenssler of Basle (Morison, pls. 32, 33) with the open type of Peter Drach of Speier (pls. 11, 34). The diamond-shaped heads and feet in some founts tend to be more pointed than in others, whilst the variations in colour or thickness of face are considerable.

Textura was the standard letter in Germany for Bibles and service books; it is the type of the 42-line Bible, the 36-line Bible, the Mainz Psalter of 1457, and of all the early Missals. It continued to be used for such books throughout the fifteenth century and occasionally after 1500. But from the time when Ratdolt returned to Augsburg in 1486 and set out to print liturgies in the Italian Rotunda, Textura began to go out of favour, and by the period of the Reformation was almost restricted to serving as a title- or heading-type. In the Netherlands and in England two descendants of the original Textura had a longer life. The Dutch variation known as the Lettersnider type (with M75 of Dr. Haebler's *Repertorium*) had been used at Cologne before 1500, and its descendants remained a rival to roman in the Netherlands for many years. The old-established firm of Enschedé of Haarlem still possesses the matrices of a fount of Textura cut by Henrik Lettersnijder of Delft about 1490, and a second set of matrices is assigned to Cornelis Hendriczoon; perhaps a son of Henrik. This second type was used in a book printed by the Brothers of the Common Life at Gouda in 1496. A third Textura of the fifteenth century in the possession of the Enschedés is considered to be of French origin. These must be among the oldest types in the world. The Lettersnider types were acquired by Johan Enschedé in 1767 at the sale of the foundry of Jan Roman en Comp (see their *Proef van Nederduitsche Letters*, Haarlem, 1925). Plantin had Flemish Texturas, of which there are reproductions in Updike, *Printing Types*, pl. 202, and in the following centuries many founts of "Flamand" or "Duits" were cut by the chief designers, such as Christopher van Dijk, Fleischman and Rosart.

Most of Caxton's books are in types of another group, but his type 3 is a Textura. One word of this type is found on the earliest sheet known to have been printed in England, the Indulgence of which a copy issued on December 13, 1476, exists in the Public Record Office.[1] Type 3 and its modification type 5, and also types 7 and 8, that is to say, one-half of Caxton's stock were Texturas, and from them are descended the stock types of the second

And be it further known by the Authority aforesaid,
That all and every of the said Exchequer Bills to be
made forth by virtue of this Act, or so many of them
as shall from ABCDEFGHIKLMNOPQRS

Fig. 2. Caslon's Textura, *c.* 1730

generation of English printers, Wynkyn de Worde and Richard Pynson. The traditional Black Letter or English used in this country and shown in most of the type-specimen books of the Caslons, the Frys and the Figgins right down to the nineteenth century, is a small Textura and differs little from De Worde's type. Among the blacks acquired by the James foundry from the Grovers and appearing in their sale catalogue of 1782, one is actually described as De Worde's, but probably in error. As to the name by which this type should be described, English is also used of a size, while black emphasises a characteristic which is shared with most other gothic types and even some romans. Mr. Morison in the introduction to his *German Incunabula* has used the word Text as the English equivalent to Textura, and he has good support for this use. Sir Hilary Jenkinson in *The Later Court Hands of England* uses the term and says that it was well established in the fourteenth and fifteenth centuries. It is the name used by the calligrapher, John Baildon, in *A Book containing divers sorts of hands*, 1571, where from the illustration there is no question as to

[1] See *The Times*, February 7, 1928.

what sort of hand is meant. It was not merely a technical term, but is found in the literary language also. In *Love's Labour's Lost*, v. 2, 42, we read: "Fair as a text B in a copybook." On that passage Prof. Dover Wilson's glossary says: "The text hand was one of the more elaborate and formal of the various Elizabethan scripts." In the use of "Church Text", the term seems to have survived among ecclesiastical artists. However, in order to avoid confusion with the term "text type", in the sense of body type, it would be safer to adopt the latinised form Textura.

The English variety of Textura has a consistent upper case with M32, although independent of the lower case (cf. the blacks shown in the Caslon specimen books). It is not so strictly without curves as the German variety. Since the English printers used it as their ordinary standard type, they needed smaller sizes than are found among early German Texturas. De Worde had one size in which twenty lines measures only 53 mm. (about 7 pt.), and with the smaller sizes the counters became less angular, otherwise they would have been choked with ink. As to its use, it was only very gradually superseded by roman. The first Bible printed in roman was of 1575, while official proclamations were commonly set in Textura in the early part of the seventeenth century. The authorised version of 1611 was printed in Textura, and an edition as late as 1647. A Common Prayer of 1687 is also in the old letter, and for law reports, its use was preserved even later. An edition of the reports of the Court of Common Pleas of 1742 is the latest recorded in the British Museum Catalogue. We may perhaps date its final disappearance as an ordinary body type at the period of the Civil War. The Oxford specimen of 1693 shows no Textura.

Group B. For the printers of Latin texts, scholastic, theological or classical, the early printers cut a less formal letter, following, of course, the manuscripts. Passing over for a moment the types of the Mainz Indulgences of 1454 and 1455, the first of these less formal designs is the Durandus type of Peter Schöffer of 1459. This is a rounder and more open letter with descenders like roman, but with neither the serifs of roman nor the feet of Textura; the descenders and the strokes which end on the line, including the long s, end bluntly; the a is open as in roman; the g has sometimes an open tail, but more often is shaped like the figure 8; the d is found in two varieties, one like roman and the other like the rounded gothic; ligatures of the round forms such as b and d with e and o are a characteristic. The effect of the increased height of the ascenders and length of the descenders is to add to the amount of white on the page and to impart a lighter appearance in comparison with Textura. There is a greater differentiation of letters and therefore increased legibility. On the other hand it still has not the full roundness of roman. Its upper case varies considerably, and in some cases is almost purely roman (see figs. 3 and 4). The letter shares some characteristics of the Renaissance and others of the Middle Ages. Hence it has been called Fere-humanistica or Gotico-antiqua. This last name was first used by Dr. Alfred Hessel in an important article, "Von der Schrift zum Druck" (*Zeitschrift des Deutschen Vereins für Buchwesen*, 1923, pp. 89 *seq.*). The hand is gothic but with considerable roman tendencies. It was the formal book-hand of the earlier Italian humanists of the fourteenth century, and in particular of Petrarch. (It has even been called Petrarcaschrift.) Petrarch was a great collector of books, and in his day the collector had also to be a calligrapher, since in many cases he had to make his own book by copying a borrowed manuscript. Petrarch himself wrote out many manuscripts and for years supported young scholars in his house, whose chief task was that of a calligrapher. Manuscripts in Petrarch's hand and in the hands of his pupils have survived, and further, there are passages in his letters in which he comments on the standard of penmanship which he desired.[1]

The group of Fere-humanisticas is by no means so well defined nor so easily recognised as the Texturas. The types differ considerably in weight and colour and the tendency towards roman is often more pronounced than in the Durandus type. The curious types used by Johannes Regiomontanus at Nuremberg and by Erhard Ratdolt in their Calendars have gone so far in that direction that they may be regarded as mixed types, belonging to neither group.

[1] Cf. *The Fleuron*, no. 7, p. 185.

The Subiaco type of Schweynheym and Pannartz has been called a Fere-humanistica, and it has also been called a roman (see below p. 38). On the other hand some types of this group tend towards the Italian Rotunda or have Bastarda elements. None the less the grouping is valid and useful in typographical description. We may describe a particular type as a Fere-humanistica with Rotunda

dei iudiciũ euadẽ posse estimemus ammonem̃
exemplo. sꝫ hoc magis sentire nos ꝯuenit. tam
diu vnũquẽqꝫ dei paciẽtiaꝫ sustentare. quã diu
pccoꝝ suoꝝ t'minũ fineqꝫ repleuerit. quo consũ-
mato eũ illico pcuti. nec illi vllam veniam iam
reseruari. Esse autẽ certũ pccoꝝ modũ atqꝫ mẽ-
surã dei ipsius testimonio ꝯprobatur. Et qꝛ vnus-
quisqꝫ vel celerius vel tardius ꝓut pccoꝝ suo-
rum modũ expleuerit iudicetur. euidẽtissime
demonstratur quãdo de sodomoꝝ ꝛ gomorreoꝝ
interitu ac incendio qui sua iam peccata cõple-
uerant ad abraham deus loquitur dicens. Cla-
mor sodomoꝝ et gomorreoꝝ ꝯpletus ẽ et peccata eoꝝ magna vehementer completa sunt.
De amorreis vero quid dicit q̃ sua nõduꝫ peccata finierãt. q̃s post multos ãnos q̃ꝫ supdicte
ciuitates cremate sũt. ꝯstat ẽẽ deletos. Nondũ
repleta sũt pcc̃a amorreoꝝ usqꝫ adhuc. Quo
exẽplo manifestissiẽ instruimur et docemur. singu-
los scd̃m pccoꝝ suoꝝ plenitudinẽ ꝯsumari. et
tãdiu ut ꝯũtãtur sustinei. quãdiu cumulũ suoꝝ
nõ habuerint delictoꝝ. Neo itaqꝫ se fallat. neo
se decipiat. malos deus nõ amat. peccatores nõ
amat. iniustos non amat. rapaces. crudeles. et
impios non amat. sꝫ amat iustos. bonos. pios.
humiles. innocẽtes. et mites. sic sc̃ptuꝫ est. Nõ
nõ deus volens iniquitatẽ tu es. Nõ habitabit
iuxta te malignus neqꝫ pmanebũt iniusti ante

Fig. 3. Fere-humanistica

Evan

Responderunt milites: mulieres nescimus · et nos ve-
lut mortui facti sumus p̄ timore angeli, Responderūt
iudei, Viuit dn̄s · quia non credimus vobis. Respō-
derūt milites. Tanta miracula videntes ihm facere n̄
credidistis · qūo nobis credituri estis? Bene quidem
dixistis. Nam vere viuit dn̄s quē crucifixistis. Audi-
uimus q̄ ioseph qui sepeliuit corpus ihu inclusistis ī
cubiculo sup clauem signato · et apientes non inueni-
stis eum · date ergo nobis ioseph quem inclusistis in
cubiculo · et nos dabimus ihm quē custodiuimus ī se
pulcro. Rn̄derunt iudei, Joseph damus nos · date vos
ihm. Joseph eni in ciuitate sua in arimathia est · et
hiesus in galilea est sicut audiuim⁹ ab angelo. Hoc
audientes iudei adinuicem dicentes timuerūt valde.

Fig. 4. Fere-humanistica.

tendencies, if for instance it has the closed a and the trapezium-shaped g of the Rotundas, and thus give a picture of the type which is more exact than that given by a vague term such as "halb-gotisch".

The history of the group is a short one, for after one generation it was superseded by the Rotundas. But between 1459 and 1485 some of the finest incunables were printed in the types of this class. The *Catholicon* of 1460, many of Gunther Zainer's books and the books of the other early Augsburg printers, and the beautiful quartos of Ulrich Zell of Cologne are examples. Schöffer had several types of this class, while Johann Mentelin of Strasbourg and the early printers of Basle followed his lead. Outside of Germany the group has fewer representatives. Gerardus de Lisa, a Fleming, printing at Treviso and other towns in the north of Italy, used a Fere-humanistica in the *Tesoro* of Brunetto Latini printed in 1475, and in a few other books.[1] In England the sole example is the first type used at Oxford by Theodoric Rood, but that is really a Cologne type, and has been identified with a type of Gerard ten Raem. In France, the gothic used by Ulrich Gering, after he had left the Sorbonne and set up in the Rue St. Jacques, was a Fere-humanistica (see Claudin, *Histoire de l'Imprimerie en France*, I, 61–3). A type of Barthélemy Buyer, the first printer at Lyons, used in 1477 in the *Miroir de la vie humaine faite par Rodorigue Hispaniol*, is of this class, but of Italian origin. It is type 99G of Wendelin of Speier, the first printer at Venice (cf. British Museum, *Catalogue of Fifteenth Century Books*, vol. V, p. 152). But oddly enough, the French appear to have been the only people who had a name for the group, the "lettre de somme". This term seems to be purely typographic and no earlier use than that of Tory in *Champ fleury* is recorded, and he does not describe the nature of the letter.[2] According to tradition it was originally used of the type of the *Summa* of St. Thomas Aquinas, of which an edition was printed by Schöffer in 1467 in Fere-humanistica. Fournier in his *Manuel*

[1] See V. Scholderer in *The Library*, December 1929, fig. 2.

[2] Wattenbach, 1896 edition, p. 297, says the term is used in the inventory of the library of the Duke of Berry, 1416; but this seems to be a mistake.

topographique uses the term vaguely of all the early standard types, including Bastardas, while the illustration which he gives of "lettre de somme" set up from actual type is in fact a small Rotunda. It appears then that in French printing offices the name had survived but not the letter. Succeeding French writers on typography, e.g. Auguste Bernard, followed by English writers, have used the name with as little exactness as Fournier. It seems that originally the "lettre de somme" was a French printer's name for our Fere-humanistica.

In recent years we have seen several revivals of Fere-humanisticas. William Morris's Troy and Chaucer types may be classed here. It is an indication of the change in the standard of legibility that Morris's archaic types have been attacked on the score of their obscurity, whereas the fifteenth-century types on which they were based were chosen as text types for the very reason that they were the most legible of the gothic hands. A second revival is the re-cutting of one of Schöffer's Fere-humanisticas by Herr Tieffenbach of the Officina Serpentis, of which a page was shown in *The Fleuron*, no. 4, p. 81, and for a third we may mention the Distel type cut for the Zilverdistel Press at The Hague. Updike (vol. II, p. 222) says it "is intended to imitate old Netherlands writing". Lastly the Ashendene re-cutting of the Subiaco type seems to justify even more than the original the inclusion of this letter among the Fere-humanisticas.

Group C. The third main group of gothic types is the Italian Rotunda or Round-text as Mr. Morison translates it. Palaeographers use the term "Bolognese letter" of a rounded letter used especially at the legal school of the University of Bologna. The variety which prevailed in Italy by the time of the introduction of printing was either derived from the Bolognese letter or closely related to it. The advertisement sheet of the calligrapher, Johann vander Hagen, includes a Textus Rotundus. Dr. Hessel has adopted Rotunda for this important group which has hitherto lacked an accepted name. German printers of the fifteenth century, e.g. the Brothers of the Common Life at Rostock, used the phrase "Litterae Venetae" of the gothic founts brought or copied from

I

Vorrede in das Bairisch lantrechtbůch.

Ir Ludwig von gottes genaden Mar/ graue tzů brandenburg. Wir Stephan. Wir Ludwig. Wir Wilhalme von gottes genadē Pfaltzgrafē bey rein vn̄ Hercz/ og in bayren ꝛc. Habē angesehen deñ ge/ prestē den wir gehabt haben in vnserem lande tzů bayren an dem rechten. Unnd dauon sey wir zů rat wordē mit vnserm herrē vn̄ vätterlein kaiser Ludwigē vō rom. Vn̄ setzen vn̄ bestättigē alles das hernach geschriben steet nach seinē gebot vn̄ haissen vnse rem land zů bairn zů fůderūg vn̄ zů sunderē genaden. Das ist geschehē do man zalt vō cristi gepurt dreüzehenhūdert vnd in dem sechsund viertzigsten jar des nächsten sams/ tags nach dem obersten ꝛc.

Wie man dz recht behaltē sol.

DA von gepieten wir bey vnseren hulden allen vn/ seren Richtern vnd Amptleüten in vnserem lande tzů bayren überal jn stetten vnd merckten vnnd auff dem land Das sy die selben recht also behalten bey iren ayden die sy vns od vnserm vicztumb darumb schweren müssen Und das sy darnach von wort zů wort. von stuck zů stucke armen vnd reichen vngeuerlich richten söllen.

¶ Das ist das rechtbůch also gancz vnd alt gepesseret. vnd auch neü artickel gesamlet. auß allen gerichten stettē vnd merckten nach des Kaisers haissen.

Fig. 5. Rotunda

Italy, that is, our Rotundas. From the British Museum *Catalogue of Fifteenth Century Books*, we find that Eucharius Silber at Rome described a small Rotunda, which he appears to have acquired from Adam Rotweil of Venice, as "littera Veneta". Venetian to a modern printer means roman in the style of Jenson, but in fifteenth-century typography Jenson's Rotundas had a much wider vogue than his roman. The name used by the Italian writing masters of the sixteenth century was "littera moderna", modern possibly as opposed to the roman, antiqua; but it may be that the name was in use at an earlier date, and that the ancient letter suggested was the pointed or formal Textura, which has a history longer by several centuries than that of the Rotunda. In contrast with Textura, Rotunda is full of curves, e.g. the b, c, d, e, h, o, etc. The feet of Textura have in part disappeared, cf. the m, the third limb of which only has a foot. In contrast with Fere-humanistica it is without the tendency to roman, the a is closed, and the ascenders and descenders are shorter. In the g the bowl often takes on the shape of a trapezium (see fig. 5). It is familiar to us in the gothics of Jenson and Ratdolt; Ratdolt's specimen sheet, so often reproduced, is convenient for reference. In Germany it makes an isolated appearance with Koelhoff at Cologne in 1472, but becomes common only in the eighties. Towards the end of the century its larger sizes vied with Textura for use as heading types and in liturgical works, while the smaller sizes took the place of the Fere-humanisticas, and finally became the stock type in Europe for theological, legal and scholastic texts. Though round, Rotunda was not so broad as Fere-humanistica and was thus more economical. There are many fine books printed in Rotunda, but it suffered degradation by the end of the century and the stock type in this style used throughout Europe, *c.* 1500, is surely the most uninteresting of all early types.

Rotunda, as we have said, was the Italian form of Textura, and in fact what may have been the first book printed in Italy was set in Rotunda. Dr. Haebler in *Die italienischen Fragmente vom Leiden Christi das älteste Druckwerk Italiens*, Munich, 1927, has described a recently discovered text in Rotunda, which he considers to have been printed in northern Italy not long after 1462. The type is connected with that of a calendar for 1462 printed at or near Vienna, and it is possible that the book also was printed there. Rotunda was also the national hand of Spain and the only gothic type of the Spanish printers. The fine bold lettering of their titles shows how well fitted Rotunda was for the purposes of display. It ultimately gave place to roman in Spain, but was revived in the Spanish Netherlands by the Imperial typographer, Christopher Plantin, who had a fine "Canon d'Espagne" cut for a Spanish Antiphonary, which was apparently never printed (cf. Updike, fig. 197). In France, up to the generation of Robert Estienne and Geofroy Tory, Rotunda was the normal type for all works in Latin, and for legal texts down to the middle of the sixteenth century. The Compagnie des Libraires at Lyons, a combine of publishers engaged principally in the production of law books, as late as 1555 printed a large folio volume of the *Consilia* of Cardinal Nicolaus de Tudeschis in this traditional letter.

In England, Rotunda was always an alien letter. Lettou's type (cf. Gordon Duff, *Fifteenth-Century English Books*, 1917, pl. xxii) was of Roman origin. Both De Worde and Pynson had small Rotundas which they used for notes with their usual Textura. The Rotundas of Robert Redman and of Thomas Berthelet were apparently the last to be used in this country. Redman's excellent type may be seen in an edition of the *Great Charter* printed by his widow, Elizabeth, in 1540. Berthelet had four Rotundas which he used down to 1544.

For these two groups (*B* and *C*), we have used two new terms borrowed from recent German studies in palaeography. The advantage of an exact nomenclature for a group of types is obvious. It is maintained that by describing a type as a Rotunda of such and such a size a fairly accurate impression can be conveyed to the reader. Dr. Hessel and other German writers have helped the study of gothic typography by giving us a working vocabulary, a vocabulary which is more economical in words and more illuminating than the vague descriptions of early types to which we have hitherto been limited. For example, Updike in his *Printing Types*

The fyrste boke. Fol.30.

NOwe lette vs retourne to the
ordre of lernyng apt for a gen-
tyll man. wherin I am of the
opinion of Quintilian / that I
wolde haue hym lerne greke &
latine autors both at one time: orels to begyn with greke / for as moche as that it is
hardest to come by: by reason of the diuer-
site of tonges/whiche be fyue in nōbre: and
all must be knowen/ or elles vneth any poet
cā be well vnderstande. And if a childe do
begyn therin at seuen yeres of age/ he may
continually lerne greke autours thre yeres/
and in the meane tyme vse the latin tonge
as a familiar lāgage: whiche in a noble mā-
nes sonne may well come to passe/ hauynge
none other persons to serue him or kepyng
hym company / but suche as can speake latine elegantly. And what doubt is there:
but so may he as sone speake good latin/as
he maye do pure frenche / whiche nowe is
broughte in to as many rules and figures/
and as longe a grāmer/ as is latin or greke.
I wyll nat contende / who amonge them/
that do write grammers of greke (whiche
nowe all most be innumerable) is the beste:
but that I referre to the discretiō of a wyse
mayster. Alway I wolde aduyse hym / nat
to de-

The fyrst lernyng in chylde-hode.

Fig. 6. Berthelet's Rotunda

says of a Rotunda of Koberger's of Nuremberg, "a type less pointed than the first gothic types" (his fig. 16); again a gotico-antiqua, according to Hessel, with bastarda elements, of Mentelin of Strasbourg (his fig. 21) is described as "semi-gothic". Ulrich Gering's first gothic, another Fere-humanistica, is "a gothic fount of transitional character". Of De Worde's Rotunda (his fig. 66),

Updike says, "the smaller has a round quality which is a little like the Italian gothic types of the time". Lettou's Rotunda (fig. 68) is "like the transitional gothic type"; Gordon Duff called this type "a small Italian gothic". Of a Rotunda of Berthelet's (fig. 281), Updike writes: "Midway between bâtarde and lettre de forme." (See fig. 6.)

Group D. The vernacular types or Bastardas.

The name Bastarda applied to a hand is found on the sheet of Johann vander Hagen, and considerably earlier, but again it has not been used in typography, except in the French variety, the "lettre bâtarde". A bastard script is current or cursive, written quickly and without the deliberation of groups A-C. It is further characterised by its descenders running down to points, including long s and f, while the ascenders are frequently looped. A typical letter is the a, which like our italic a, is what the Germans call "einstöckiges", one-storeyed; the g has the tail open. The earliest founts of this group are the small types of the Mainz Indulgences of 1454 and 1455, one of them being more thoroughly bastarda than the other; the 30-line Indulgence has s and f with pointed descenders, the 31-line has not. German early Bastardas vary considerably in respect of pointedness and of colour. The type of Hans Schönsperger's *Sachsenspiegel*, Augsburg, 1482, is a black and round letter, while that of Koberger's German Bible, Nuremberg, 1483, is more pointed and much lighter in colour. The first has more in common with Schwabacher and the second with the later Fraktur.

The Bastardas, or at least the gothic Bastardas, were confined to the countries north of the Alps, and the chief variety outside Germany was the national French hand, the "lettre bâtarde" (see fig. 7). The inventory of the library of Charles V made early in the fifteenth century, already referred to, offers examples of the use of the term. All books in French were written in this bâtarde, and when Pasquier Bonhomme printed at Paris in 1477 *Les grandes croniques de France*, he naturally cut a "lettre bâtarde" for the text. The long series of popular books in the vernacular published by Antoine Vérard are all in this letter, and as late as 1530 we find

Lacteur

Prologue declaratif de la matiere
de ce present liure
appelle le faulcō.

Pour faire passer tēps aux sei/
gneurs dames escuiers et damoi/
selles q̄ voulētiers oyent parler du
deduit de chiēs doiseaulx ⁊ damours
Jay entreprins mectre par escript vng
cas puis certain temps aduenu en frā
ce de deux gracieux amoureux. Cest/
assauoir vng hōneste gentil hōme Et
vne noble damoiselle Lesquelx cōbien
quilz sentraymassent leaulmēt eurēt

Fig. 7. Lettre Bâtarde

Simon Du Bois printing devotional works of a Protestant tendency in bâtarde. Du Bois was employed by Geofroy Tory to print one of his Books of Hours in bâtarde in 1527, but Tory's own book *Champ fleury*, in which a plate of the "lettre bâtarde" is shown, is set in roman, although written in French. Even after 1530 many French books, especially romances, were still set in bâtarde by printers like the Bonfons at Paris, and Claude Nourry and Oliver Arnoullet at Lyons. However, the Renaissance hands won their way in France, and we find that Jean de Tournes, who began printing in 1542 at Lyons, had no bâtarde nor any other gothic types. Fournier's bâtarde shown in the eighteenth century was an historical curiosity.

In design this French hand has all the characteristics of Bastarda as described above. It belongs to the rounded rather than the pointed group, and has one characteristic letter in the lower case, the initial v with a superimposed loop. The upper case varies considerably and is often not different from the upper case of a Rotunda. The letter is found also in the other French-speaking countries; for example, at Geneva and at Antwerp, and even in Germany. Marcus Reinhard, a German who had worked at Lyons, printed at Kircheim in Alsace from 1490 with a French bâtarde, Books of Hours in Latin and even tracts in the German language. In the Netherlands there was also a local variety of this northern Bastarda, the Burgundian, of which a fine example was used at Bruges by Colard Mansion about 1476 in *La Controversie de noblesse*, and several other books. Caxton's *The Recuyell of the Historyes of Troy*, the first book printed in the English language, is set in a similar type, known as Caxton's type 1, less restrained and altogether inferior. Caxton's second type, with which he began to print in England, is again of the same family, but marred by the excessive number of its loops, by many bad-combining letters and a miserable w. French printers needed no w, and English printers, having no model before them, failed for many years to design this letter in a satisfactory manner. These Burgundian Bastardas, familiar to us in the majority of Caxton's books, and in the books of the St. Albans printer, are of historical interest, but as types quite the worst of their class. Pynson did better when he introduced the French "lettre bâtarde" and his *Dives et Pauper*, 1493, set in this letter, is one of the best English incunables. Caxton's Burgundians did not survive into the sixteenth century, and the French "lettre bâtarde" persisted only in editions of the Statutes and legal works, often written in Norman-French. Rastell's *Grete Abridgement*, printed about 1535 by Robert Redman, is one of the latest examples. The bâtarde can be traced in the books of Thomas Berthelet, who had two founts and used them not only in law books, but in many of his general publications, down to 1543.

The French "lettre bâtarde" then passed out of use about the middle of the sixteenth century; but in Germany the Bastarda has remained the national type, at first in the variety known as Schwabacher, and afterwards in the more familiar Fraktur.

SCHWABACHER

The particular variety of Bastarda used by Friedrich Creussner at Nuremberg from 1485 (his type 4) became the most popular German type for books in the vernacular and received the name of Schwabacher. From a passage quoted in the *Archiv für Geschichte des Deutschen Buchhandels*, vol. x, p. 142, it appears that the term was in common use among printers by 1576, and must have originated many years earlier. Why the little town of Schwabach in Bavaria, where there was no printing or typefounding in early days, should have given its name to this group, has not been satisfactorily explained. (See fig. 8.)

Schwabacher has the usual Bastarda characteristics, the closed, one-storeyed a, and pointed descenders to s and f; the tail of the g is open; the b, d and h are sometimes looped and sometimes not. The design of the upper case as well as that of the lower case is fixed, with some few variations. In all the earlier gothic founts the variations among majuscules are so numerous as to defy classification. The upper case was a separate fount, often revealing little attempt at harmony with the lower case. But with these later Bastardas we can take account of the capitals also in defining groups. In fact the group called the Upper-Rhine type is in its later

Ode Saphica Endecaſillaba dicolos tetraſtrophos conradi celtis proſpho netice et ſinbuletice. Ad fridericuz ter cium inuictiſſimum.

Phebe ripheos aditure montes
Explicans noctem breuioris vmbris
Lenta ſub celo rigidis reformas
Gramina campis
Thaurus arctoo propior coluro
Oritur tecum referens tepores
Cum vagas ſentit pliades aduri
Lumine phebi
Repparat vultus roſeo decore
Mundus: et plauſtrũ ſinuans vtrũq;
Anguis algorem poſiturus optat
Sole nouari
Terra profuſo madidans humore
Parturit letos rubicunda flores
Nauigant ſtrato relegendo merces
Equore naute
Non minax vaſto boreas egeo
Obuius ſeuit violenter auſtro
Sorte luctando timida mouentes
Prelia ponto
Sed per extremas agitatus oras
Spirat in terris Zephirus tepenti
Suſtitans flatu taciti ſepulta
Semina mũdi
Sentiunt gratas animata curas
Fedus aſciſcunt ſobulis creande
Qua ſub eterno ſtabilitur orbis
Temporis euo

Fig. 8. Schwabacher

history distinguished from Schwabacher by variations in some few capitals only. In Schwabacher the M is Haebler's M81; other traditional capitals are A and S. Finally in colour, throughout its history, the letter was essentially black.

There were roughly only three sizes of Schwabacher, of which the middle size, about 90 mm. to twenty lines, or 12 to 13 pt., was the usual standard type. The larger size, about 106 mm. or 15 to 16 pt., was used for folio Bibles and historical works, e.g. those of Heinrich Steyner of Augsburg with the Weiditz illustrations, and to a large extent also for news-tracts. The smaller size, about 78 mm., is perhaps less common. It is remarkable that we do not find gradations up from the 11 pt. to the 16 pt., but three definite groups in size. There are, of course, exceptions, e.g. Köpfel at Strasbourg printed in 1538 a Bible in double columns in a Schwabacher measuring only 46 mm. to 20 lines.

Of the three German Bastardas which preceded Fraktur, Schwabacher was easily the most widespread. In Nuremberg, where it originated, it is all but universal. Johann Stuchs was the only printer of any importance who used an Upper-Rhine type from 1528. In Augsburg the standard types are divided about equally between Schwabacher and Upper-Rhine types. In the towns where the Upper-Rhine type, e.g. Strasbourg, or the Wittenberg letter predominated, we always find as well Schwabachers of the middle size, while for the smaller and larger sizes Schwabacher was almost the only vernacular type. The letter was occasionally used in the Netherlands, e.g. by Cornelis Hendriczoon at Delft in a *Nieuw Testament*, 1524 (a curiously light design), and by Johan Hoochstraten at Antwerp in Bugenhagen's *Souter*, 1526. The few English books extant, printed wholly or in part in Schwabacher, were probably printed abroad.

Schwabacher, together with its variant the Upper-Rhine type, remained the standard German text type down to about 1550. It was a quarter of a century before Fraktur became at all common except in headings. In the second half of the century Schwabacher gradually declined into its ultimate position of a secondary type, used in much the same way as italic was used with roman. German type-specimens of the seventeenth and eighteenth centuries continued to show Schwabachers along with the Frakturs, but in much smaller numbers. One result of its neglect in comparison with Fraktur was that the original design remained undisturbed. Whilst the popular letter was subjected to various experiments, ending in the pallid faces cut by Unger, the Schwabacher of the eighteenth century had changed little from the first fount of 1485. Unger, in fact, expressed a violent dislike to this letter and declined to concern himself with it; for purposes of emphasis he recommended wide spacing rather than the employment of Schwabacher. The Enschedés' specimen, *Die hochdeutschen Schriften*, 1919, illustrates the development of Schwabacher for several centuries. In the latest example shown, that of the Leipzig type-founder, Breitkopf, dated 1765, there is a certain refining of the thin strokes; but the only specimen in which any attempt is evident of experimenting with the traditional design is an eighteenth-century type, Corpus in size, which is described as of unknown origin. German printers of today have revived Schwabacher, and it is now being used to a greater extent than at any time since the sixteenth century.

THE UPPER-RHINE TYPE

The second definite group of Bastardas has in modern days been given the name of the Upper-Rhine type from the district in which it originated, and was principally used. The earliest founts of the class are found with Ludwig Renchen at Cologne (1484), with Peter Schöffer at Mainz, the Breidenbach type, and with Johann Grueninger at Strasbourg in the same year as the first Schwabacher, 1485. In the lower case the design differs from that of Schwabacher by the presence of more looped ascenders; in the upper case the chief distinguishing letter is the M, Haebler's M44. In fact the M is the test letter, by the presence of which a type is included in the group. The H is only exceptionally the usual Schwabacher form. In size nearly all Upper-Rhine types are about 90 mm. to 20 lines, never much smaller and only rarely of a large size. Sigmund Grim at Augsburg had a fount of this class measuring 111 mm., but usually the larger founts were pure Schwabachers.

This grouping is not altogether satisfactory, because in fact the Upper-Rhine type is not essentially different in design from Schwabacher. J. Wegener in *Die deutsche oberrheinische Type*, 1909, has traced the group down to 1550, taking as his basis M44, and many of the founts in his list differ from Schwabachers solely by the occurrence of this M. Even in the fifteenth century we find a type like that of Conrad Kachelhofen at Leipzig (see *Ein Buechlein von dem Sterben*, 1494), which is simply a Schwabacher with M44. The looped ascenders found in Schöffer's and Grueninger's types tend to be eliminated, with the result that the lower cases of these two Bastardas becomes identical. Grueninger certainly kept his looped ascenders down to the end of his career in 1532, but the majority of the sixteenth-century Upper-Rhine types are not especially marked off from Schwabacher in this respect. The Upper-Rhine type is a convenient sub-group within the larger Schwabacher group. It seems probable that to a sixteenth-century printer, who had not heard of M44, a type of this group would have been known as a Schwabacher.

As its name implies, this Bastarda was used principally in the Rhineland towns from Mainz southwards, with a few examples at Cologne. It was common at Basle and is found in the books of Christopher Froschouer of Zürich.

THE WITTENBERG LETTER

The next Bastarda group is a genuine classification with some marked differences in design. It was of much more local use than the others, and mainly confined to Wittenberg and the neighbourhood, whence the name. The design appears first at Leipzig at the press of Melchior Lotter, his type 11, in 1508. The younger Lotter used the type at Wittenberg. The M is Haebler's M48. In the lower case the distinguishing characteristic is the shortness of the ascenders, resulting in a comparatively large-faced type. Besides the Lotters, including Michael Lotter at Magdeburg, Jacob Thanner at Leipzig (1510), M. Sachse at Erfurt (1525) and M. Blum

Vnnd ap wol/hertzog Heinrich/bis an dieſe czeit/alles was ſich czu
recht vnd billichkeit eygent/gegen mir vbergãgen. Hab ich mich doch
vorſehen/er wurde ſich ſchemen vff bloſſen vnerfintlichen wortten/ane
bewerung czubeharren/vnnd des grundt czubefinden. Als der durch-
leucht hochgeborne furſt vnd her. her Georg hertzog czu Sachſſen rc.
Mein gnediger herre/ſampt genanten hertzog Heinrich/in iren ſachē/
von Biſchoffen. Prelaten/Graffen. Ritterſchafft. vnd Stetten dieſzer
lande etzliche perſonen am Mitwoch nach ſandt Bartholomeus tag
czur Numburg. verſamelt gehabt/vff die czeit/hab ich mich ſchriftlich
erbotten/vor denſelben/mein gnedigen gunſtigen hern vnd freundenn/
desmals/ von hertzog Heinrichen bewerung ſeiner/mir vffgelegkten/
ertichten wort/czugewartten/im auch/vmb alles anders/was er wider mich vffczubringen wiſſe/antwort/vnd alles was mir von Ere vnd
rechtswegen eygent/czupflegen. Es iſt aber vonn hertzog Heinrichen
nicht angenomē/wie beſtendig ſeine wort daraus befunden/wie rum-
lich ſein begynnenn czuachten iſt/las ich in aller fromen menſchenn be-
trachtung bleiben. Vnnd iſt mir leydt/an im czubefinden/des ſich bis
an dieſe czeit/alle andere erliebende menſchen geſchemet. Als auch her-
czog Heinrich vor dieſer czeit/vff mein vleyſſig anſuchenn/ſeins vffle-
gens halben/mir vor ſeinen Reten/recht tzupflegen/geweygert/wye in
nechſten meiner ſchrifft/ſo ich vor dieſer/hab auſgehen laſſenn/clerlich
angeczeit iſt/ich auch in derſelben ſchrifft vil vbergleiche rechtsbiettung

Fig. 9. Wittenberg Letter

at Leipzig (1537) had the type. There were two copies, No. 1 being used from 1524 by H. Emser's printer at Dresden and by Cranach and Döring at Wittenberg. In this copy the lower case was much the same, but the capitals differ, notably the A, G, O, R, T and Z. The other Wittenberg printers had a close copy of the Cranach and Döring design, and it was this type which was so widely used in Saxony and Thuringia. It is found in Berlin, in Breslau in 1541, and in Copenhagen from 1559.[1] Wittenberg letters vary little in size, they measure round about 95 mm. to 20 lines, that is to say, they are much the same size as the medium sizes of Schwabacher and Upper-Rhine type. The fact that the Wittenberg letter looks bigger is a matter of height of ascenders. For the same reason a page in this letter has an unusually close-set appearance (see fig. 9).

FRAKTUR

The fourth Bastarda group is the last to appear in type, but historically the most important. The sheet of Vander Hagen shows that a hand called Fraktur, meaning broken, was in use before 1450, and Wattenbach gives instances of earlier uses. The hand in the design to which it had evolved early in the sixteenth century was also called "Kanzleischrift". In modern days it has been called "gebrochenes" in an attempt to avoid a Latin word, and also "Deutsch". Certainly no type has a better claim to be called "The German Letter". The writing master, Johann Neudörffer, who showed the letter in his calligraphic books, gives some account in his *Nachrichten* of 1547 of the early Fraktur types. From him we learn that the designer of one of the first Frakturs, the Teuerdankschrift, was Vincenz Rockner, and the cutter Hieronymus Andreae, Formschneider, afterwards Duerer's printer. Duerer was certainly closely connected with the originators of the new Bastarda, but there is no evidence that any of the designs are due to him. His three last books, *Underweyssung der Messung*, 1525, *Etliche Underricht zu Befestigung der Stett*, 1527, and the *Vier buecher von menschlicher Proportion*, 1528, are all printed in Fraktur, and in the

[1] See Nielson, *Dansk typografisk Atlas*, pls. xxx, xli, xlviii and lxxiv. See also *The Library*, June–Sept. 1943, pp. 61–5.

Underweyssung, he shows a Textur with a decided leaning towards Fraktur. Neudörffer says also that he himself designed a Fraktur for Formschneider.[1]

In design Fraktur is a narrow and pointed letter. The lower case is foreshadowed by some Bastardas of the fifteenth century (cf. fig. 19 in Updike). There is a marked difference from Schwabacher in the width of the letters and also in the serif formation of the ascenders. In Schwabacher the b, for example, if not looped, ends bluntly, but in Fraktur the ascender runs up to a point. The upper case is essentially a calligraphic letter, further removed from early gothic than is Schwabacher. The loose ends of the capitals have been aptly called by the Germans "Schnörkel", elephants' trunks. The comparison is certainly helpful. The net result of these Schnörkel and of the pointed ascenders in the lower case is a spiky and restless design and a design decidedly inferior to Schwabacher. Two reasons may be given for the ultimate defeat of the better design by Fraktur. Just as Rotundas had driven Fere-humanisticas out of the printing offices, because they were more economical of space, so again the narrower Fraktur appealed to the printer's pocket. The second reason is that the printers after 1550 actually seem to have preferred the fussiness of the new letter. The exaggerated use of it on title-pages is evidence of this preference.

Between 1513 and 1524 eight varieties of Fraktur were cut. First were the three cut for the Emperor Maximilian's printer, Hans Schönsperger, of Augsburg. We have already mentioned that one was designed by Vincenz Rockner and cut by Hieronymus Andreae. The first, known as the Gebetbuch type, was used for the *Liber Horarum ad vsum Ordinis Sancti Georgii*, which appeared on December 30, 1513, from Schönsperger's press. R. Kautzsch in his

[1] There is preserved in the library at Augsburg a MS. writing book by Leonhard Wagner, entitled *Proba centum scripturarum*, in which two leaves show hands like the two first Fraktur types. They appear under the odd name of Clipalicana. K. F. Bauer in *Leonhard Wagner der Schöpfer der Fraktur*, Frankfurt, 1936, maintains that these hands were the models followed by the type designers. He dates the MS. 1507–10. But Carl Wehmer in the *Beiträge zur Inkunabelkunde*, N.F., no. 11, 1938, holds that the MS. was not completed until 1517, and that Wagner was following the type designer.

Entstehung der Frakturschrift, 1921, suggests that Schönsperger may have cut this first design. The second, the Teuerdankschrift, appeared in 1517, and in the same year also we find the third and smallest, the Gilgengartschrift. The fourth in date is the unusual type, in two sizes, of Grim and Wirsung at Augsburg (Proctor's types 12 and 14). In 1522 appeared the first Fraktur in the design which became traditional, that of Hieronymus Andreae of Nuremberg, designed by Neudörffer. The text on Duerer's *Triumphwagen*, dated 1522, is in this type, and later Duerer used it for the three books already mentioned (see fig. 10). Lastly, in 1524 we have the designs of Cranach and Döring at Wittenberg, that of Wolfgang Köpfel at Strasbourg, and that of Johann Petri at Nuremberg.

In spite of these eight designs it was quite a generation before Fraktur became a serious rival to Schwabacher as a text type. The three types of Schönsperger rapidly became popular as heading types, but there are few books printed wholly in any one of them. The Gebetbuch type was naturally from its size unsuitable for any purpose except headings. Steyner's later edition of the *Teuerdank*, 1537, is printed in Schwabacher. The Gilgengartschrift was used for Schönsperger's New Testament of 1523 and again in Luther's *Ain betbuchlein* of the same year. It is found also in at least two unsigned books of Steyner's, *Anzaygendt Newzeyttunng wie aygendtlich mitt der schlacht von Pavia . . . gefallen ist*, 1525, and in 1538 in *Von der erpärmlichen ellenden hartwiderpringlichen auch der gantzen Christenheit*, etc. Melchior Ramminger took the strange course of using the upper case of the Gilgengartschrift with the lower case of his usual Upper-Rhine type (see his edition of Luther, *Vonn dem hailigen leyden Christi*, 1524, and many other tracts). Grim and Wirsung used their Fraktur only till 1522, for the most part in signed works; their unsigned Luther tracts were printed in Schwabacher.

Turning to the Nuremberg Frakturs, the assumption that Duerer's printer was Hieronymus Andreae, Formschneider, is borne out by the fact that some of the editions of Duerer's works printed in the years following his death, set in the same types, bear

Durchleuchtigister großmechtiger Künig genedigster her/Von wegen der
genad vnnd guetthat / so mir von weilond dem aller durchleuchtigisten
vnd großmechtigen Kayser Maximilian hochlöblicher gedechtniß ewer
Maiestat herren vnd großvater beschehen ist/ erken ich mich der selbenn
nit minder dan gemelter Kayserlichen Maiestat nach meinem geringen
vermügen zudienen schuldig sein/Dieweil sich nun zu dregt das E. Mt.
etlich steet vnnd flecken zu befestigenn verchsafft hat/ bin ich verursacht
meinen geringen verstandt derhalb an zuzeygen/ ob E. Mt. gefellig sein
wolt / etwas darauß ab zunemen/Dann ich dar für halt / ob mein an-
zeygen nit an allen orten angenommenn werd/ müg dannoch züm teil
was nutz daraus entspringen / nit alleyn E. Mt. sonder auch andern
Fürsten/ herrn/ vnnd stetten/ die sich geren vor gewalt vnd vnpilliger be-
drangung schützen wolten/pit darauff gantz vnterteniglich. E Mt. wölle
die erzeygung diser meiner dinstparkeyt genediglich von mir annemenn
vnnd mein genedigster herr seyn.

E. K. Mt.

Fig. 10. Nuremberg Fraktur, 1522

his name; for instance, the Latin edition, *De varietate figurarum et flexuris*, 1532, has the imprint "Impensis viduae Durerianae per H. Formschneyder". Further, other books printed in the same types (there were five sizes) contain Formschneider's imprint, for example, Hans Gerle's *Musica Teusch auf die Instrument*, 1532, and a book well known for its wood-cuts by Michael Ostendorfer, *Warhafftige beschreibung des andern Zugs in Osterreich*, Gedruckt zu Nuremberg durch Hieronimum Formschneyder, 1539. Besides a number of unsigned books in the same Fraktur, there is one book, *Eyn wunderliche Weyssagung von dem Bapstum*, which reads in the colophon "Gedruckt durch Hans Guldenmundt". Other books printed by Guldenmundt are in Schwabacher.

The second Nuremberg printer who designed Fraktur was Johann Petri. In 1525 he issued a printer's specimen-sheet showing besides his other types three sizes of his new design. The two smaller sizes had already appeared in a Psalter of 1524, a reprint of the Wittenberg Psalter of the same year. The largest size, a 36 pt., rather like the Gebetbuch type, was without capitals, and appears as the main text in, I believe, only one book. *Der Psalter teutsch* of 1525 is perhaps the most remarkable of all the early books in Fraktur. The headings are in Petri's second size, about 14 pt., and the capitals belong to a Rotunda. This type is not included by Crous and Kirchner[1] in their list of early Frakturs. Of other books printed entirely in the second there are the *Türcken belegerung der statt Wien*, 1529, and a Hans Sachs, *All Römisch Kaiser nach ordnung*, etc., unsigned. The smallest size appears as the main text in *Burgermeister von alter her bin ich genant*, unsigned. As heading type, Petri made use of the Gebetbuch type rather than his own design.

According to Crous the Wittenberg Psalter in Luther's translation of 1524 was printed by Cranach and Döring. The type appears again in an unsigned book of 1525, B. Gretzinger's *Eyn vnüberwintlich beschirmbüchlyn*, but only for the register. *Die Epistel an die Colosser*, of 1527, bearing the imprint of Simphorian Reinhart, is set entirely in this Wittenberg Fraktur.

[1] *Die gotischen Schriftarten*, 1928.

Wolf Köpffel, of Strasbourg, printed a New Testament in 1524 in a Fraktur measuring 95 mm. to 20 lines. Some of the type appears on the title-page of Caspar Hedio's *Von dem zehenden zwo predig bescheen im Munster* and in Catharine Zell's *Entschuldigung*, etc., both of the same year. In January of 1525 Christoph Rudolff's *Behend vnnd hübsch Rechnung* is set entirely in the Fraktur; but at no time did Köpffel make more than occasional use of the type.[1]

The Wittenberg and Strasbourg Frakturs were like the design of Formschneider of Nuremberg which, as we have said, became the traditional Fraktur. When Sigismund Feyerabend at Frankfurt in 1560 printed the German Bible in Fraktur, Schwabacher was doomed. By that date Frankfurt had become the centre of the German book-trade, and the publications of Feyerabend show that Fraktur had become the fashionable type for books in the German language.

Even before it became the normal text type, Fraktur had won popularity as a heading type. The type designers exaggerated the Schnörkel of the upper case for the purpose of decorating title-pages. But this exaggeration was not found to be enough, and full satisfaction could only be obtained by cutting the titles on wood. Crowded title-pages are familiar in seventeenth-century English books, but the lack of restraint implicit in Fraktur allowed the German printers to go a step further and to produce the very worst title-pages in the history of the book. The lower case was subjected to various experiments in condensation and in enlarging

[1] Other printers who used Frakturs as text types by 1535 were Mathias Apiarius at Strasbourg from 1531 (see several tracts by Martin Bucer), Georg Ulrich at Strasbourg (see *Die new welt, der landschaften vnnd Insulen*, etc., 1534, a book printed in double columns in a small size of Fraktur, twenty lines measuring only 71 mm.), Melchior Lotter at Leipzig (see G. Wicelius *Sieben psalmen*, 1534, and other tracts by Wicelius. The same type was used by Hans Lufft (see *Auslegung D. M. Luthers vber den Sechs vnd dreissigst Capitel des Propheten Esaias*, 1535), whilst N. Schirlentz used a larger size in *Ausschreibunge eines heiligen freyen Christlichen Concilij*, 1535), and lastly Weygand Han at Frankfurt (see Johann Adelphus's *Keyser Friderichs des Ersten . . . löblich geschichten*, 1535).

the face, in much the same fashion as that introduced by the Dutch with their roman types. Thus in the specimen of Frakturs issued by the Luther foundry at Frankfurt in 1678 we find a *Grosse* Fraktur, that is, a letter of a large face in comparison with its body. This is the "gros œil" fashion which we refer to below in dealing with roman types. In the specimen of 1768, issued at Frankfurt by the widow of J. H. Schippelius, one Fraktur is described as *Lange*, that is condensed, and another as *Runde*, a description which seems to be a contradiction in terms when applied to this letter. However, the design in general was not radically altered, and the best founders of the eighteenth century, like Breitkopf at Leipzig and Haas at Basle, observed the original tradition handed down from Formschneider. It is not until we reach Unger that any serious attack was made on the letter.

Johann Friedrich Unger (1753–1804) was at first a woodcutter. He became a printer at Berlin in 1780, and added a type foundry to his business about the year 1790. He started with matrices acquired in part from the Luther foundry, and also from Firmin Didot of Paris. His introduction of the modern-face roman of Didot into Germany is described below. The first specimen of his work as a type designer appeared in 1793, *Probe einer neuen Art Deutscher Lettern*, with a second edition in 1794. In the introduction Unger gives an account of his experiments and intentions with regard to Fraktur. He says that he had conceived the idea of reforming the letter eight years ago. His friend, Firmin Didot, made three attempts to carry out his idea of a reformed Fraktur, but none of them proved satisfactory. Finally he had himself to undertake the laborious task of learning to cut types, and with the help of his assistant, Gubitz, succeeded in producing two different designs. He tells us that his purpose was to round off the corners of the lower case and to remove the gothic "Schnörkel" of the upper case. He remarks also that some letters of the traditional Fraktur are not sufficiently differentiated; there is confusion between the b and d, n and u, and V and B. Further, he says that he tried to borrow the "Helle und Zarte" of the Latin scripts. As to the result, he had no great success in his own day and, except in Germany, has received little commendation from writers on typographical history, perhaps less than he deserves. Updike dismisses him very briefly, and Mr. Morison refers to his design as a "pallid abomination". The Unger Frakturs have come into the possession of the Enschedés and are excellently displayed in their specimen *Die hochdeutschen Schriften*. They show two sizes described as "Erster Versuch" and the later design, as well as one of Didot's experiments. The Didot and the Cicero "Erster Versuch" are so exotic that one can understand their rejection. The Petit Fraktur "Erster Versuch" has some unusual capitals, notably the A and the G, whilst the capitals of the later design are more according to the tradition. Unger rejected these capitals, no doubt, because they were unusual, and not because they were less legible. There is little to be said for Fraktur on the score of legibility, and one of the few facts established by modern tests of the legibility of types is that the German letter is less easily read than roman. The controversy, still continued in Germany, between the claims of Fraktur and of roman, rests on nationalist grounds. Unger at any rate did make a Fraktur as legible as any hitherto cut; in fact, by smoothing out the angles of the lower case he approached more nearly to the despised design, Schwabacher. But in colour he went to the other extreme and by copying the lightness of roman produced the pallidness which is the chief ground of complaint against him. It was in this way principally that he left his mark on future typography. Frakturs of the nineteenth century are definitely more pallid than the earlier designs.

CHAPTER TWO

Roman

THE VENETIANS AND OLD-FACE GROUP

OUR ROMAN TYPES are based on the book hand of the Renaissance humanists, which was developed, principally at Florence, in the first half of the fifteenth century. The hand is known as "humanistic" or "neo-caroline", and when translated into type received the name of "littera antiqua". Although in 1450 it was the most modern of letters, yet it was derived from a script, the Carolingian, which was more ancient than any gothic descendant. Our name roman, taken from the French, is perhaps as good as antiqua. The upper case at least is pure roman and the lower case is an immediate descendant. However, the name probably originated from the fact that the first roman used in France, that of the Sorbonne press of 1470, was copied from the fount of Schweynheym and Pannartz used at Rome from 1467. As against three main groups of gothic, there are only two divisions of roman, the formal and the bastard, otherwise italic. Formal romans fall into three families succeeding one another chronologically, fifteenth-century, old-face and modern-face romans. These divisions are well known, but recent researches have thrown some light on the historical origins and the development of the second and third groups.

When Schweynheym and Pannartz began printing Latin texts at Subiaco it was natural that they should copy the letter then in favour with the Italian humanists. It has been said that the type they produced has semi-gothic characteristics, but it has been demonstrated by Mr. Morison[1] that they were closely following their calligraphic models and that we may call the type the first roman without qualification. It was formerly held that the earliest roman was that of Adolf Rusch at Strasbourg. This supposition was based on the occurrence of a date, 1464, in MS. in a copy of Durandus's *Rationale divinorum officiorum* printed by Rusch, which is in the Basle library. It has now been shown that the date is a mistake for 1474, and that no book by Rusch in roman can be dated earlier than 1467.[2] When the printers moved to Rome in 1467, they designed a new fount, a roman with the full serif formation, but still with some angularity in letters like the e. Of the first roman used at Venice, that of Johannes da Spira, it may be said that it was the best so far cut, but rather spoilt by a very heavy upper case, a fault found in many later romans.

Within the first decade of the history of roman types we reach the design of Nicolas Jenson, 1470, which has frequently been re-cut and has been the most highly praised of all romans (see fig. 11). The excellent composing qualities of his letters and their evenness in colour have been particularly commended, and Jenson seems to have understood that these points are of greater importance even than the design of individual letters. In fact some of his letters are not above reproach. Mr. Morison[3] has criticised the ugliness of his straight-shanked h, a form introduced by Jenson, and the undue height of his capitals. As to the h, at least the new form differentiates that letter from the b. Erhard Ratdolt, Venice, 1476, preferred the earlier h. The g also is by no means a perfect letter, and several of the capitals, apart altogether from their size, are poor in design, for instance, the M with its slab serifs, and the Q. But in spite of these defects in details, to be convinced that the Jenson roman deserves all the praises that have been lavished on it,

[1] See "Early Humanistic Script and the First Roman Type", *The Library*, June-September 1943, pp. 1–29.

[2] See V. Scholderer, "Adolf Rusch and the Earliest Roman Types", *The Library*, 1939, pp. 43–50.

[3] "Towards an Ideal Type", *The Fleuron*, no. 2, pp. 57–75.

CHABRIADIS VITA.

CHABRIAS ATHENIENSIS HIC
quoq; in ſummis habitus ē ducibus:
reſq; multas memoria dignas geſſit.
Sed ex his eluc& maxime inuentum
eius ĩ prœlio quod apud thebas fecit:
cum boetiis ſubſidio ueniſſ&. Nanq;
in ea uictoria fidentem ſummum ducem Ageſilaum
fugatis iam ab eo cõducticiis cateruis reliquã phalangẽ
loco uetuit cedere: obnixoq; genu ſcuto ꝓiectaq; haſta
impetum excipere hoſtium docuit. Id nouũ Ageſilaus
intuens progredi nõ eſt auſus: ſuoſq; iam incurrentes
tuba reuocauit. Hoc uſq; eo græcia fama celebratũ ẽ: ut
illo ſtatu Chabrias ſibi ſtatuã fieri uoluerit: quæ publice
ei ab atheniẽſibus in foro cõſtituta eſt. Ex quo factum
ẽ ut poſtea Athletæ cæteriq; artifices his ſtatibus ſtatuis
ponendis uterentur cũ uictoriã eſſent adepti. Chabrias
autem multa in europa bella adminiſtrauit. Cum dux
atheniẽſiũ eſſ&: in ægypto ſua ſpõte geſſit. Nã Nepte-
nabum adiutum profectus regnum ei conſtituit. Fecit
idẽ cypri: ſed publice ab atheniẽſibus Euagoræ adiutor
datus: neq; prius inde diſceſſit q̃ totam inſulam bello
deuinceret. Qua ex re athenienſes magnam gloriã ſunt.
adepti. Interim bellũ inter ægyptios & perſas cõflatũ ẽ:

Fig. 11. Jenson's Roman

one has only to open one of his folios. There is certainly something satisfying about his page.

Individuality of type design, which is a characteristic of the Incunable period, is as pronounced among the early romans as in any one group of gothic types. But from the time of Jenson until about 1495 no printer designed a roman which is of great importance for the historical development of this letter. Some printers reverted to mixed types, like the Ptolemy design of Leonard Holle of Ulm. This roman, perhaps modelled on the humanistic hand of Nicolaus Germanus, the editor of the Ptolemy of 1482, has a gothic g and a rather angular e. Others designed more calligraphic founts, like that of Gerardus de Lisa at Treviso; the g and the y, the unusually long ascenders and descenders, and the rather exaggerated serifs of this type are closer to the humanistic hand than the Jenson model.[1]

That the roman types of Aldus Manutius represent the beginnings of the old-face group is the discovery of Mr. Morison, and a discovery of some importance for the understanding of the evolution of type forms. The statement that Garamond took Jenson's roman as his model, a statement frequently repeated in the histories of printing, has stood in the way of a correct view of the origins of our principal book type. Mr. Morison[2] has examined Aldus's roman in its various states, and has found that where it differs from Jenson it agrees with Garamond. The type of the Poliphilus is comparatively condensed—it is characteristic of early romans that they consume much space—the capitals are both narrower and shorter, the lower case e has a horizontal straight to the eye, as against the oblique straight of Jenson. All these points are found in Robert Estienne's first Garamond, and when in addition we find in Garamond an M with no serif on the right limb and a G with a serif extending to the inside only, and that these rather peculiar forms occur in the capitals used in the *De Ætna* of Pietro Bembo,

[1] For a reproduction see V. Scholderer's article in *The Library*, December 1929, fig. 3.

[2] "The Type of the Hypnerotomachia Poliphili", in the *Gutenberg Festschrift*, 1925.

printed in 1495 in an earlier state of the Poliphilus roman (see fig. 12), the supposition that Garamond modelled his design on that of Aldus becomes a certainty. It may be noted that the Aldine capitals are inscriptional, like the lettering of classical Rome as

PETRI BEMBI DE AETNA AD
ANGELVM CHABRIELEM
LIBER.

Factum a nobis pueris eſt, et quidem ſe-
dulo Angele; quod meminiſſe te certo
ſcio; ut fructus ſtudiorum noſtrorum,
quos ferebat illa aetas nõ tam maturos, q̃
uberes, ſemper tibi aliquos promeremus:
nam ſiue dolebas aliquid, ſiue gaudebas;
quae duo ſunt tenerorum animorum ma
xime propriae affectiones; continuo ha-
bebas aliquid a me, quod legeres, uel gra-
tulationis, uel conſolationis; imbecillum
tu quidem illud, et tenue; ſicuti naſcentia
omnia, et incipientia; ſed tamen quod eſſet ſatis amplum futurum argumentum
amoris ſummi erga te mei. Verum poſtea, q̃ annis creſcentibus et ſtudia, et iudi
cium increuere; nóſq; totos tradidimus
graecis magiſtris erudiendos; remiſſiores
paulatim facti ſumus ad ſcribendum, ac
iam etiam minus quotidie audentiores.

Fig. 12. Aldine Roman

found, for instance, on the Arch of Trajan. The slab serifs of Jenson's M and of the A and N of other early romans are now discarded. Our upper case is the only literally roman letter among our types. It seems probable that Aldus himself was not especially interested in the design of roman letters—his interest was in Greek literature and in the publication of the classics—and that the chief credit should be given to his type-cutter, Francesco Griffo, an account of whom is given below. When Robert Proctor condemned the Aldine founts, Greek, roman and italic, he was unfair as to the roman, prejudiced probably by his justifiable objection to the Aldine Greek.

It is significant that Aldus had no gothic types. In Italy, by his day, there were only two classes of books which tradition required to be set in Rotunda, law books and Liturgies. But in other countries, where the revival of learning followed at least a generation behind, the new Renaissance letter was far less popular. By 1480 only ten roman founts are recorded in the presses of Germany. Their number began to increase rapidly after 1490, the printers of Basle in particular leading the way. Basle has been called the gateway by which the new learning entered Germany. Johann Amerbach, the leading printer there in the nineties, had learnt to print in Venice and had several roman types in the Venetian style. Similarly, the only printer in the Netherlands who used roman in the fifteenth century, Johann von Paderborn at Louvain (1474–96), had also worked at Venice. In other cases the influence of humanistic scholars can be traced in the introduction of roman types, where the readers were hardly ready for them. Two professors of the Sorbonne, Guillaume Fichet and Johann Heynlin, in 1470 brought the first printers into France, Ulrich Gering of Constance, Martin Kranz and Michael Friburger of Colmar. Their press was set up in the college and their type was roman, modelled on that which Sweynheym and Pannartz were using at Rome. The first book printed, the *Epistolae* of an Italian Renaissance scholar, Gasparinus Barzizius, was a text intended for students of Latin. When Gering and his partners had left the Sorbonne and set up their press in the Rue St. Jacques, they soon returned to the native gothic. It was not till after 1500 that the tide began to turn in favour of roman, again under the influence of a student of the new learning. Josse Badius, before he began to print at Paris, had studied at Italian universities and had been a press-corrector for Johann Trechsel at Lyons. Badius and his contemporary Henri Estienne, the first printer of that famous family, led the new fashion in France and prepared the way for Tory and Garamond. In Spain, as in France, printing begins with a roman type and afterwards the native gothic prevails. Lambert Palmart, a Fleming, in 1474 printed at Valencia the *Obres e Trobes* of Fenollar in a roman type, but his example was not followed. The great majority of Spanish incunables and even of the books printed in the first

Oratio quam erat habiturus Petrus Gryphus:
Sędis Apoſtolicę prothonotarius/ac iterū nūcius:
Ad Sereniſſimū Hēricū.vij.Anglię Regē: Ni para
tā expoſitionē immatura Regis mors preueniſſet.
SIqui ſunt fortaſſe Sereniſſime ac Inuictiſſi
me Rex/Siqui inquam fortaſſe ſūt/qui nō
ex mediocritate mea/ſed ex Maximi San=
ctiſſimiq; Pontificis/a quo venio/ſumma dignita=
te:et ex tuæ Maieſtatis ſingulari eximiaq; præſtan
tia/hunc meum ad te aduentum metiātur:expecta
re eos quidem arbitror/me primo hoc cōgreſſu ita

Fig. 13. Pynson's Roman

quarter of the sixteenth century were set in Rotunda. The few books printed in roman were generally the works of scholars interested in the new learning, such as Antonio de Lebrixa.

The roman, or as our early printers sometimes called it, the white letter, first appeared in England in 1509, and again was more probably due to the author of the book than to the enterprise of the printer. Petrus Gryphus of Pisa came to England as papal collector in February 1509. He remained there for three years, and on his return to Italy in 1512 was made Bishop of Forli. The speech which he was to have delivered at his audience before Henry VII was never spoken, owing to the death of the king, but he had the *Oratio* printed by Richard Pynson in a roman type. The dedication is dated "Idibus Maii", so that the speech may be supposed to have preceded two other books of the same year, in which the type is found, a Savonarola tract, *Sermo Fratris Hieronymi*, with a preface dated October 8, and Alexander Barclay's translation of the *Ship of Fools*, issued on December 13. The type is used for the half-title only of the Savonarola, and for the Latin text of the *Ship of Fools*, the English being in Textura. Pynson's roman was used by Antonius Venetus at Paris in 1502; both this and the very similar letter used by Wynkyn de Worde from 1523[1] closely resemble contemporary French romans, for instance that of Josse Badius at Paris. The lower case is not very good, and the upper case distinctly poor. The smaller roman of De Worde used from 1520 (20 lines=81 mm.) is better, and we may compare it with the type which Geofroy Tory used for his *Champ fleury* and the majority of his books. One roman of this class has survived to our day, and is part of the wonderful collection of early types owned by the Enschedé of Haarlem. In the specimen of this roman issued in 1926 they attribute it to Peter Schöffer of Mainz, and consider it to be the oldest type in their collection. It came to the Haarlem firm in 1768 from one Jacobus Scheffers, a printer at Bois-le-Duc, a descendant of the Schöffers. Their dating of the type is too early, but it is at least early sixteenth century. It is first found at Cologne in 1527.[2] The third roman used in England was that of the Cambridge printer, John Siberch, or Johannes Laer de Siborch, in which he printed some ten books in the years 1521 and 1522. This roman was perhaps cut in Cologne. Siberch's roman appears condensed, but this seems to be due to the narrow bodies of the letters rather than to a condensed face; the c, however, is actually narrow in face. It may be noted that Siberch's g is without the rudimentary stroke—the ear—at the top right-hand corner, which has persisted by the force of tradition with but few exceptions.

The fact that English printers did ultimately adopt roman as their standard type seems to be almost accidental. We have noted above that Textura was still regularly employed in the seventeenth century in certain classes of books. English black letter might very

[1] See Isaac, *English and Scottish Printing Types*, vol. I, figs. 11 and 12.
[2] See Reed's *Old English Letter Foundries*, new ed., 1952, p. 88.

well be the normal letter today for books in the vernacular, just as Fraktur is in Germany. We have no black letter versus roman dispute, perhaps because in the sixteenth century our printers were conscious of their inferiority to continental printers, in particular the French, whose lead they followed. There was no English standard to be maintained. The German printers on the other hand did not forget that they had been the first to develop the art, and were naturally inclined to resist foreign innovations, at least when printing in their own language.

If the connection between "Garamond" and fifteenth-century romans was obscure, there was equal obscurity until recently as to the history of the Garamond founts themselves. The account given by earlier textbooks ran somewhat as follows: "Garamond took Jenson as the model for his new roman; about 1540 he cut several sizes of roman and italic for the King's foundry." The 1540 was due to the Imprimerie Royale who in 1845 labelled their "caractères de l'université" as "Garamond 1540". The existence of these "caractères," called Garamond on such high authority, spread confusion, since the types could not be found in any sixteenth-century book. The story that Louis Luce revised the letters in the eighteenth century is probably due to this state of uncertainty. Mrs. Warde's (Paul Beaujon) happy discovery that these famous "caractères" were not Garamond's and not even of the sixteenth century, but were cut by Jean Jannon, printer at Sedan and Paris, who issued his specimen in 1621, has cleared the way and made it possible to give a reasonable account of the Garamond roman.

In her article on Garamond which appeared in no. 5 of *The Fleuron*, Mrs. Warde has traced the new roman back to the year 1531. In that and the following year at least four printers at Paris had their "Garamond" founts. Simon de Colines printed with his Terentianus fount, so called from an edition of the *De literis Horati* of Terentianus Maurus, finished in November 1531. Colines seems to have been experimenting with the design of roman for some years; editions of the Greek medical writer, Galen, printed in 1528 show a roman which except for a few letters is the same as the type of 1531. Even as early as 1525 the roman in which the first Tory Book of Hours was printed is an advance on the types which Colines had acquired from Henri Estienne.

The Terentianus version had already been used in two little tracts by Guillaume Bochetel, describing the entry of Queen Leonora into Paris and her coronation, issued in March and May of the same year, and published by Geofroy Tory. But

G N

Vertere Mecœnas, vlmiſque adiungere vites
Cōueniat: quæ cura boum, quis cultus habēdo
Sit pecori: atq; apibus quāta experiētia parcis:
Hinc canere incipiā. Vos ô clariſſima mundi
Lumina, labentem cælo quæ ducitis annum:
Liber, & alma Ceres, veſtro ſi munere tellus
Chaoniam pingui glandem mutauit ariſta:
Poculáque inuentis Acheloia miſcuit vuis:

Fig. 14. Garamond Roman

already in January 1531[1] had appeared Robert Estienne's first book in his new roman in three sizes, the *Isagoge* of Jacques Dubois. While cutting the new sorts required for this philological work, Estienne seems to have taken the opportunity to revise the whole alphabet. In 1532 his Virgil (see fig. 14), dated September, and his handsome folio Bible, finished in November, were printed in the new letter. In March 1532 Antoine Augereau issued the *Orationes* of Andrea Navagero in his version of the revised roman, and a fourth version was used, also in 1532, by Chrestien Wechel. These four related founts cannot have been cut by one man, but that one at least was the work of Claude Garamond seems almost

[1] That the date of this book is 1531, and not 1532, appears from E. Armstrong's *Robert Estienne*, Cambridge, 1954. Other books of 1531 in the new romans are there cited.

certain. The most important of the four, historically, was Estienne's, and this is the particular "Garamond" referred to above as being derived from the Aldine romans. The lower case became the traditional French roman, and by the end of the century had the widest popularity throughout Europe. The upper case was revised about 1550, taller capitals were cut, and the unusual G and M disappeared. After this revision we get the letter shown in the specimen sheet of the Egenolff-Berner foundry at Frankfurt issued in 1592, which displays seven sizes of "romain de Garamond". Mrs. Warde suggests that Antoine Augereau, whose new roman is closely akin to Estienne's, may have been the engraver of the type used in the Dubois. Augereau[1] was an engraver of types, if we may trust Lacaille, and the shortness of his career—he was burnt as a Protestant and printer of suspected books in 1534—may account for the obscurity of his name. On the other hand, as Mrs. Warde shows, in the *Juvencus* published by Garamond himself in 1545, and in other books printed by the men especially connected with him, his son-in-law, Pierre Gaultier, and his partner, Jean Barbé, the Estienne fount was taken as a model. Further, the roman capitals of the middle size of Garamond's "grecs du roi" are the capitals of the Estienne fount (the capitals of the largest size which first appeared in 1550 are the revised capitals as in the Egenolff sheet). Either then Garamond cut the Estienne fount or he accepted it as his model. At all events he won credit with posterity for the design, as the Egenolff sheet testifies.

In the Dubois and in Estienne's folio Bible of 1532 three sizes of the new roman appear; the largest, Gros Canon, excellently displayed in the preliminaries of the Bible, has an historical importance of its own. Hitherto the lower case had not been cut in very large sizes and titles had been composed either in capitals or partly in Rotunda. But after the appearance of this Gros Canon, large sizes of lower case "Garamond" became fashionable on

[1] See J. Veyrin-Forrer, "Antoine Augereau", Paris, 1957, in *Paris et Ile-de-France*. It seems that Garamond had been apprenticed to Augereau. The article includes reproductions of Augereau's types.

titles. The title-pages of almost any French printer of the middle years of the century illustrate the point; perhaps none better than those of Jean de Tournes. Especially his large folios, the Bible in French, 1551, the Serlio, 1551, the Jacques Bassentin, 1557, and the Jean Duvet, 1561, are magnificent examples of the styles. The Italians followed suit, and in one case at any rate we know that a French type designer, Guillaume Le Bé, who was working at Venice in 1545, cut a Canon roman for Torrentino of Florence. This letter is shown in his "Spécimens de caractères Hébreux, grecs, Latins . . . gravés à Venise et à Paris (1545–92)", of which a facsimile was published in 1889 by Henri Omont. In England we find a similar title type used by Thomas Berthelet; see *A Necessary Doctrine for any Christian man*, 1543.

By the end of the century the Garamond roman had become the standard European type. French romans were purchased by Paolo Manuzio at Venice about 1557 for use in the books of the newly established Academia Veneta. Christopher Plantin at Antwerp bought types at the Garamond sale, and many of his other romans were influenced by Garamond.[1] The Paris designs were taken to Frankfurt by André Wechel, who bought part of the Garamond foundry at the sale of his stock in 1561. We have already referred to the specimen of the Egenolff-Berner foundry at Frankfurt issued in 1592. This foundry under the Luthers was the most important in Germany in the seventeenth century, and continued to display their Garamond romans in all their Latin specimens of 1622, 1664, 1702, 1718 and 1745, sometimes omitting the name of Garamond. Two centuries after Garamond's death a European printer could buy his types, nor would they have appeared as archaic revivals, though not quite in the latest fashion. The Luthers sold types in the Netherlands also. Charles Enschedé has shown that almost all the roman and italic letters displayed in the specimen of Johann Elzevier of Leyden, 1658, came from their foundry, and that a considerable number of them were those shown in the Frankfurt sheet of 1592.

[1] Cf. Harry Carter, "The Types of Christopher Plantin", *The Library*, September 1956, with a sheet of reproductions.

The roman typography of the seventeenth century differed very little from that of the sixteenth, at least for the body types. Large and heavy capitals were used for titles, and there were considerable changes in the formula for book production, but in the history of the development of type-forms the century is almost a blank. The Imprimerie Royale, established at Paris in 1640 by Cardinal Richelieu, began with types of the Garamond style, which came perhaps from the press of Sebastien Cramoisy, the first director of the Press. In 1642 the Jannon types were acquired and these with the original Cramoisy types fulfilled the needs of the Press down to the end of the century. The Jannon roman was also a copy of Garamond, but had some peculiarities of its own. Mrs. Warde in the introduction to her reproduction of the Jannon specimen has pointed out that the top serifs of the m, n, p and r are conspicuously pointed up, a peculiarity repeated in the modern copies of the "Caractères de l'Université".

In this century the Dutch book trade enjoyed its most prosperous days. The publishing and printing firm of the Elzeviers became the most famous in Europe. But neither the Leyden branch, nor the Amsterdam branch of this house, cut their own types. As already said, they were largely supplied by the Luther foundry, and the famous Dutch foundries of Cristoffel van Dijk and the Voskens were not established until 1648 and 1641 respectively. Their romans are a heavier version of the Garamond design, with stout serifs and an avoidance of anything exaggerated. The Dutch founders made their counters sufficiently large to escape any risk of choking with ink; the eye of the Garamond e, for instance, is dangerously small. Their descenders tended to be shorter and in the course of time a new style was developed of large-faced romans with distinctly abbreviated descenders. By the end of the century prefatory matter in particular was often set in large sizes of these Dutch "gros œil" as the French called them.[1] Updike says they have a rolling effect. Such

[1] On types of a large x-height, see S. Morison, "Leipzig as a Centre of Typefounding", *Signature*, no. 11, 1939, and A. F. Johnson, "The Goût Hollandais", *The Library*, 1939.

types are common in both German and English books as well as Dutch.

Turning back to trace the story of roman types in England, we find that Thomas Berthelet was using a lower case like Garamond's by 1534 (see Isaac's *English Types, 1503–58*, fig. 67). In the second half of the century French romans were in very general use. In two articles in *The Library* (June and September 1933) Col. Isaac summarised the Elizabethan romans and italics and traced them all back to continental sources. He found that the majority of them are to be found on the Egenolff-Berner sheet, 1592, or on Plantin's *Index Characterum*, 1567, or on both. There is no exception even in the case of John Day, who was so highly praised by Reed. Day's boasted double pica roman and italic, at a later date to be used in the London Polyglot Bible, came from the Low Countries. Reed's remark that the Polyglot was "wholly the impression of English types" is far from the truth. The number of English types, that is to say, types cut by English designers, before the generation of Nicholls and Moxon, must be very small. The earliest known specimen of types set up by an English printer, dating from about 1650 (reproduced in Berry and Johnson's *English Type Specimen Books*) displayed only foreign types.

It is commonly asserted that in the century preceding Caslon, Dutch types were much used in England. Joseph Moxon, in his *Mechanick Exercises*, 1683, regards the Dutch as the only possible models, and the Edinburgh printer, James Watson, in his *History of Printing*, 1715, includes a display of Dutch types. There are two series of letters extant which further illustrate their popularity, those of Thomas Marshall written to Bishop Fell from 1670–72, and those of Thomas James to his brother John, written in 1710. Marshall's letters were published by Horace Hart in *Notes on a Century of Typography at the University Press, Oxford*, 1900. Marshall was preacher to the English merchants in Holland and was employed by the Bishop to visit the Dutch foundries with a view to making purchases for the University Press. Thomas James visited Holland as a founder in 1710 and was treated with some suspicion as a competitor. Incidentally we learn from his letters that the London printer, Jacob Tonson, had recently spent a large sum of money in the purchase of Dutch types. James dealt mainly with Johannes Rolu of Amsterdam, who had issued his *Proeven van Letteren* shortly before James's visit. These Dutch types are shown in the catalogue of the sale of the James foundry in 1782.[1]

But this assertion about Dutch types needs modification. Types or matrices may have been bought in Holland and yet be derived from French punches in the possession of a German foundry, namely the Luthers at Frankfurt. It has already been noted that much of the Elzevier material came from that house, and the same is true of some of the purchases made by Thomas Marshall for Bishop Fell. Several of the smaller sizes of roman and italic in the Oxford specimen of 1693 appear to be identical with those of the Frankfurt sheet of 1592.[2]

Such English types as were cut during this period were in the Dutch style and generally very bad in technique. One characteristically English roman may be mentioned. In 1679 a Herodotus in Greek and Latin was printed in London "typis E. Horton et J. Grover". As Grover was a founder it is possible that the type was of his own casting, if not also of his design. The book is set in double columns and the roman is a light and condensed letter, a curious forerunner of Fleischman. Probably it was designed for this very purpose, for the setting of a text in narrow columns. However, similar condensed types of a smaller size are found as early as 1648; perhaps they were first cut in connection with newspaper printing, for the "Mercuries" of the Civil War period. Attention may be called to two of the capitals; the U is of the same form as the lower case u, a practice common in the seventeenth century and almost limited to that century. The R has the curly

[1] See Reed, *op. cit.*, new edition, pp. 220–2, where a list of the exotic types is given, Rolu's being marked with the initial R.

[2] Important discoveries have recently been made at Oxford on the Fell types, but results have not yet been published. It has been established that the larger sizes were cut at Oxford by their own founder, Peter Walpergen.

tail which is generally considered to be typical of eighteenth-century types. In fact such R's are often found in English books from about 1640. It will be met with in an Oxford type, described in the specimen of 1693 as "Great Primer Roman and Italic cut by Mr. Nicholls, not good", and not shown there; a deliberate omission made good in Horace Hart's book. Another English type which had a considerable vogue was Moxon's Canon roman. This was used not only by Moxon himself, but fairly generally as a heading type in books and also in newspapers. The type was later acquired by William Caslon and is one of the few types displayed on the Caslon specimen sheet of 1734, which was not cut by Caslon himself. The only other type of Moxon's of historical interest was his Irish fount, the story of which may be read in Reed (new edition, pp. 175–8).[1]

The last of the distinguished type designers who were, consciously or unconsciously, pupils of Garamond was William Caslon. If Caslon had ever seen or heard of the "romains du roi" he was entirely uninfluenced by that modern type or by the subsequent work of Fleischman, Luce and Fournier. Born in 1696, he was about five years younger than Fleischman, but to the end of his life he ignored the new developments in type-forms introduced by the continental founders. His specimen of 1764 might have been produced a hundred years earlier. Caslon was originally a gunsmith; the punches which he cut for lettering on bindings attracted the notice of printers who persuaded him to turn his attention to letter-founding. His first type was an Arabic, cut in 1720, and was followed by a roman, according to John Nichols, cut in 1722 (cf. Reed, new edition, pp. 231, 232). It was not until 1734 that a sufficient number of letters had been cut to justify the printing of a specimen sheet. By that time the Caslon roman was accepted as the best English book type and its popularity was such that in the lifetime of the designer there was no competition. In Reed's *Old English Letter Foundries* will be found a number of contemporary references which testify to Caslon's success, and among his admirers was Baskerville. He stopped the importation of Dutch

[1] See also E. W. Lynam in the *The Library*, March 1924.

types, and even the Oxford Press could not rely on the Fell types only; the Press was buying Caslon types from 1742.[1]

Caslon took as his model the best Dutch types of the seventeenth century, and his roman has been praised for the qualities of homeliness and common sense which are found in the roman of Van Dijk. If the function of type is to be a medium and to efface itself, the Caslon roman achieved that end. The letters are pleasantly legible, combine together well, and no one letter calls attention to itself by any oddity of form. All the letters are not equally good in detail, more particularly in the upper case. The rather dumpy A and broad M are in some sizes not good. But the fact remains that the type in composition is pleasing and eminently serviceable. However, Caslon was not better than the designers he took as models. He owes his success in England, not to any originality, but to the fact that he was the first really competent engraver and caster of types in this country.

[1] See J. S. G. Simmons, "The Undated Oxford Broadsheet Specimen", *The Library*, March 1956.

CHAPTER THREE

Roman

THE EVOLUTION OF THE MODERN FACE

DURING THE EIGHTEENTH century the design of our roman types underwent a radical change, resulting in the style which we know as modern face, the type of the nineteenth century and still the type used in newspapers and many of our books. It therefore becomes important to define what we mean by modern face. A roman which embodies the three following characteristics: (*a*) flat and unbracketed serifs, (*b*) abrupt and exaggerated modelling, (*c*) vertical shading, we shall call modern face. Flat serifs, though not unknown in the history of calligraphy, were an innovation in typography about the year 1700; hitherto they had invariably been inclined, and further triangular; that is to say, the under part of the serif was not parallel to the upper part. The modelling, that is the gradation from the thick part of the stroke to the thin part, had been gradual. The thickest part of the round letters, such as c, e, g and o, did not come at the middle of the down stroke, but slightly below the middle, or, in the o and g, the two thickened parts were not horizontally opposite each other, but more or less diagonally opposite. This meant that the angle of shading ran diagonally, more or less, across the page, and not vertically up and down. This is in accordance with a script made with a pen held at an angle, the natural way. If an O is written with a broad-nibbed pen held at an angle, it will be seen that the thickest lines are diagonally opposite.

In fact the old-face roman, based on a hand-drawn letter, still shows traces of that origin. By the year 1700, the professional calligrapher, whose work was reproduced on copper-engraved plates, had begun to hold the pen at right angles to the paper, to produce vertical shading, and to reduce their thin strokes to hair-lines. In a study of Baskerville roman by Mrs. Warde, published in *The Monotype Recorder*, September-October 1927, this point was illustrated by a plate from George Shelley's *Alphabets in All Hands*, *c.* 1715, and Mrs. Warde pointed out that Baskerville, a writing-master in his earlier days, was translating into type a style that was already in vogue among the calligraphers. The whole question of the evolution of roman from old style to modern face is largely a question of technique, rather than the rejection of one design for another on a definite principle. In typography we shall find that mechanical improvements in the printing press and changes in the texture of paper allowed the engraver of types to produce effects which would have been impossible in early days. It was useless for a Garamond to cut a delicately modelled serif which the processes of reproduction available would have obscured.

The normal nineteenth-century type is modern face, showing all the characteristics of our definition, often with additional aggravations. Apart altogether from fat-faced types, the habit of producing condensed types in the modern style has made much nineteenth-century typography even more unpleasing than it need have been. The narrow capital M, for instance, of the average modern face, illustrates the tendency at its worst. The exaggerated and abrupt modelling, coupled with mathematically vertical shading, resulted in a rigid and mechanical letter which was an abomination to men like William Morris. If one may judge by the typography of our leading printers of today, one may conclude that there are few of our typographers who would defend this modern face. If we confine the term modern face to such types, it becomes difficult to label many types of the eighteenth century except by some such vague and unsatisfactory epithet as transitional. How many of the characteristics of modern face are to be present in a type before it can be classified as such? Serifs may be flat, but still bracketed;

shading may be vertical in part, that is, vertical in some round letters and not in others, and may be accompanied by modelling of various degrees of exaggeration. Any decision must be somewhat arbitrary.

Towards the end of the seventeenth century it was decided that a new series of roman and italic types should be cut for the exclusive use of the Imprimerie Royale, of which Jean Anisson had recently become director. The aid of the Académie des Sciences was called in, and in 1692 a committee of experts was appointed, with Jaugeon as chairman. A lengthy report was presented in which an elaborate construction of each letter, on a mathematical basis, was attempted. One of the squares, divided and subdivided into 2,304 small squares, which was to control the construction of each letter, was reproduced in Arthur Christian's *Débuts de l'imprimerie en France*, 1905. The account of Jaugeon in that book is set in the "Caractères Jaugeon", cut in 1904 by Hénaffe. From this re-cutting it becomes clear that Philippe Grandjean, the engraver of the Imprimerie, followed the design recommended in the report; probably he ignored the theory. By 1702 the sizes first cut were ready and the types were used for the printing of the *Médailles sur les principaux évènements du règne de Louis le Grand*. This roman has flat, unbracketed serifs, and on the ascenders of the lower case the serifs run across to the right as well as to the left. The shading is more vertical and the modelling rather more than in the old face. On the left side of the l, there is a small flick, such as at one time had been usual in gothic types. Here it was probably adopted as a distinguishing mark, and this was perhaps also the reason for the cross serifs. We may note also the bottom serif to the b, the flat bottom serif to the u, and the curly-tailed eighteenth-century R (see fig. 15). The modern face is implicit in this design, and yet to a casual observer, it would appear old face. This is because the modelling is only slightly more pronounced and because there are no hair-lines. Technique was not yet sufficiently advanced to allow of the true modern face. The modernness of the design is perhaps more evident when it is used with modern methods of printing. For example, in the Abbé de Liebersac's *Discours sur les monumens publics*, 1775, printed with Anisson-Duperon's improved press,

Il pose ce fondement tant de son histoire que de a doctrine et de ses lois. Après, il nous fait voir tous es hommes renfermés en un seul homme, et sa femme nême tirée de lui; la concorde des mariages et la ociété du genre humain établie sur ce fondement; a perfection et la puissance de l'homme, tant qu'il orte l'image de Dieu en entier; son empire sur les nimaux; son innocence tout ensemble et sa félicité lans le Paradis, dont la mémoire s'est conservée dans 'âge d'or des poètes; le précepte divin donné à nos remiers parents; la malice de l'esprit tentateur, et on apparition sous la forme du serpent; la faute l'Adam et d'Eve, funeste à leur postérité; le premier omme justement puni dans tous ses enfants, et le enre humain maudit de Dieu; la première promesse le la rédemption, et la victoire future des hommes ur le démon qui les a perdus.

La terre commence à se remplir, et les crimes 'augmentent. Cain, le premier enfant d'Adam et d'Eve, ait voir au monde naissant la première action tragique; t la vertu commence dès-lors à être persécutée par e vice. Là paraissent les caractères opposés des frères, 'innocence d'Abel, sa vie pastorale, et ses offrandes

Fig. 15. "Romain du Roi"

and the modern revivals by Arthur Christian in his *Débuts de l'Imprimerie*, 1905.

Type-founders were forbidden to copy these "romains du roi". Consequently many romans cut by Paris engravers at later dates were less modern than this Grandjean design. But that the types of the Imprimerie were in fact copied, we know from Pierre Cot's *Essais de Caractères d'Imprimerie*, Paris, 1707, a little specimen of Oriental and Greek types; the descriptions of the types shown are set in a roman which has all the characteristic features of the "romain du roi".[1] We have also the evidence of Pierre François Didot le jeune. In 1783 that printer was accused of imitating these types, and in his defence protested against the injustice of his being accused, whereas he was only a printer and several type-founders had for years shown designs like the "romains du roi". He instances Sanlecque in 1742 and says that the same types afterwards appeared in the specimen books of Gando. He says that Madame Hérissant had printed Réaumur's *Histoire des Insectes* in a type of this style in 1742, and admits that he himself had used another in Houel's *Voyage de Sicile*, of which the first volume had appeared in 1782.[2] The type of the Houel has in fact flat serifs, the double serifs and even the flick on the l. Pierre Didot l'ainé has something to say about Grandjean and Alexandre, his successor, in the notes to his *Épître sur les progrès de l'imprimerie*, 1786. "Leurs caractères romains sont à-peu-près imités de ceux de Garamond pour la forme de la lettre; seulement ils l'ont chargé de traits horizontaux qui la défigurent." To Didot, who was then printing with the modern types of his brother Firmin, the "romains du roi" were not much removed from old face.

Grandjean's work was continued by Jean Alexandre, and finally completed by Louis Luce, who cut the smallest size, perle—there were in all twenty-one sizes of roman and italic. Luce, in addition to his work as punch cutter to the Imprimerie Royale, cut on his own account a number of other romans displayed in his *Essai d'une Nouvelle Typographie*, 1771. In the "Avertissement" of this

[1] A facsimile was published in 1924 by D. C. McMurtrie.

[2] See Bernard, *Histoire de l'Imprimerie Royale*, 1867, pp. 96, 97.

specimen Luce explains wherein his types differ from the "romains du roi". He says that his serifs are on the left side only and that they are inclined (as a matter of fact in the larger sizes they are flat). He gives as a reason for preferring the inclined serif that such was the natural stroke of the pen, and that types are derived from the hands of the calligraphers. He says, further, that his letters are more oval, that is to say more condensed, and guards himself from the charge of copying the Dutch by pointing to the delicacy of the serifs and the general harmony of his types. This is the most striking characteristic of the Luce romans, their condensation. He declares that he had published proofs of his types in 1732 and complains that his ideas had been stolen. There is clearly here an allusion to Pierre Simon Fournier, who copied not only the Luce ornaments, shown in the little specimen of the "perle" roman and italic of 1740, but also his roman and italic. Fournier was the better designer, but the idea of his "poétique", a condensed letter intended for the printing of the long verses of the French Alexandrine without breaking into a second line, was derived from Luce (see fig. 16).

Fournier was an industrious worker and offered his customers, not one St. Augustin or Cicero roman, but a whole family on the same body, all cut by himself. He has "petit œil", "œil moyen", "œil ordinaire", "gros œil", "œil serré" and "œil poétique". The "petit œil" is a small-faced type with comparatively long ascenders and descenders. This, says Fournier, leaves a greater interval between the lines, is therefore lighter in appearance but fatiguing to the eye. The "œil moyen" is heavier, therefore more readable; the "gros œil", or large face, is still heavier. In the "œil serré", or condensed face, the letters are a little less round and therefore more letters can be set in one line; the "œil poétique" is also "serré", but made lighter by lengthening the descenders. Fournier's ordinary roman, that is to say, neither "gros œil", "petit œil" nor "goût Hollandais", but yet somewhat condensed, a type which has been re-cut of late years by the Monotype Corporation, may be looked at as an example of a transitional roman of the eighteenth century. Some small points are taken from Grandjean, such as the curly-tailed R, the b, d and u with flat bottom serifs. But on the other hand the top serifs are not flat, nor is the shading vertical (consider the e). There is more "modernity" about the upper case, but on the whole the type impresses one

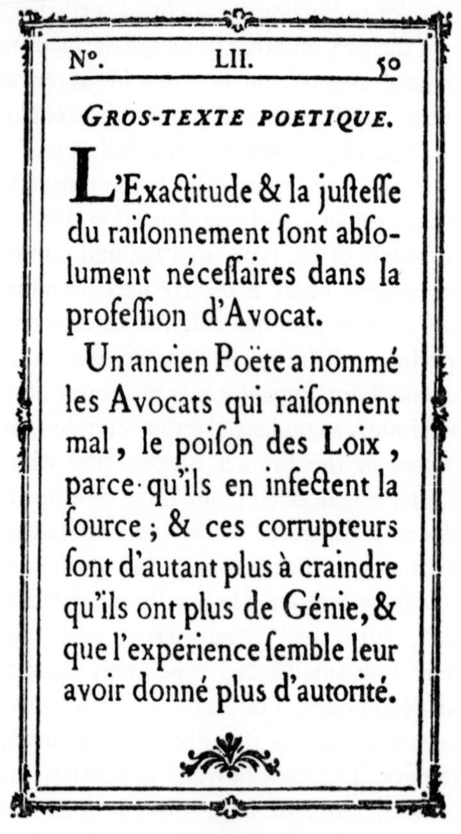

N°. LII. 50

GROS-TEXTE POETIQUE.

L'Exactitude & la juſteſſe du raiſonnement ſont abſolument néceſſaires dans la profeſſion d'Avocat.

Un ancien Poëte a nommé les Avocats qui raiſonnent mal, le poiſon des Loix, parce qu'ils en infectent la ſource; & ces corrupteurs ſont d'autant plus à craindre qu'ils ont plus de Génie, & que l'expérience ſemble leur avoir donné plus d'autorité.

Fig. 16. Fournier's Poétique

rather as an old face. Both Fournier and Luce were more "modern" in their treatment of italic.

Of the "gros œil" and the "goût Hollandais", Fournier says: "Les Hollandais ont imaginé de faire ces sortes de caractères gros œil, maigres et alongis." He is thinking of the distinguished type-founder, Johann Michel Fleischman, a German who worked in Holland (see fig. 17.) He was a famous man in his day, but is now

Text Romyn.

Lors qu'Aspasie étoit concubine d'Artaxerxès : On ne sauroit lui donner moins de vingt ans à la mort de Cyrus : elle avoit donc soixante - quinze ans lors qu'un nouveau Roi la demande comme une grace particuliere. PLTGA

ABCDEFHIJKMNOQSU
VWXYZÆ ÆÀBCDEFGHIJKL
MMNOPQRSTUVWYZ ÇĒŌ℣℟
12345678910†([§!?

Text Cursyf.

Ciceron menagea toûjours Dolabella le plus doucement qu'il put. Il avoit sans doute plus d'habileté que de fermeté, & il voioit que le parti de Pompée se ruïnoit de plus en plus par les contiuelles victoires de Jules

ABCDEFGHIKLMNO
PQRSTVWXYZ. UJÆ

Fig. 17. Fleischman's Roman and Italic

somewhat under a cloud. Updike says that he took the life out of all his types and can find nothing good to say of him. But his light and rather condensed St. Augustin roman, cut as early as 1732 and acquired by the Wetsteins, and later by Enschedé, was very popular in Holland, and not without reason. At any rate, when given every advantage of good printing, such as it receives in Charles Enschedé's book—it is there used for the whole text—it appears not unworthy of the praise which Johan Enschedé gives it. The Leipzig founder, Breitkopf, in his *Nachricht von der Stempelschneiderey*, 1777, in reviewing the Enschedé specimen, praises Fournier as against Fleischman, and says that the condensed letters are a mistake. It is evident that Louis Luce and Fournier derived their taste for condensed romans from Fleischman. The "gros œil" itself, that is large-faced types with short descenders, were also very much "goût Hollandais" (see above, p. 49). The second famous Dutch type-cutter of this period, J. F. Rosart, was also employed by the Enschedés, especially for the cutting of roman capitals. Those shown in figs. 275–8 of Charles Enschedé's book are entirely modern, and it may here be remarked that thin, flat serifs and vertical shading in capitals are frequently found in the first half of the eighteenth century, when the lower case was still in the state of transition. The specimens of capitals issued by the Luther firm at Frankfurt in 1716 and again in 1718 offer examples.

The house of Didot is one of the illustrious families in the annals of typography. About the year 1789 there were no less than seven members of the family engaged in the various branches of the book trade at Paris, the two brothers François Ambroise (retired in 1789) with his two sons, and Pierre François with three sons. The elder branch, l'ainé, was the more important, and the most important member of the family from our point of view was F. A. Didot's younger son, Firmin (1764–1836). The father, F. A. Didot, was both printer and type-founder, and among other appointments which he held was that of printer to the Comte d'Artois, afterwards Charles IX, whilst his brother, P. F., was printer to Monsieur, the King's eldest brother, afterwards Louis XVIII. This royal patronage had doubtless its part in encouraging the cutting of new types. A. F. Didot (see his *Essai sur la typographie*, 1852) says that one Waflard engraved the first types of his grandfather, F. A. Didot. This Waflard, or Pierre Louis Vaflard, is mentioned by Lottin as a type-founder and pupil of Gando. But there seems to be no record of any actual type cut by him, and possibly this man has been given too much prominence in the history of the Didot types. In Thibaudeau's *Lettre de l'Imprimerie*, reproductions of Waflard's types are given (pl. 15, 16), but there seems to be no authority for the attribution. They are more probably Firmin Didot's types. There is further uncertainty in the textbooks as to the dates of the first new Didot types. M. Marius Audin, in *Le Livre*, 1924, and Updike say about 1775. The letter to the *Mercure de France* quoted in Audin, pp. 73, 74, appeared in 1783. The writer, Anisson, director of the Imprimerie Royale, extols Garamond and Baskerville as against the new Didot letters (see Coyecque, *Collection d'Anisson*, vol. II, p. 450). In that year F. A. Didot printed three French classics in quarto, seven volumes in all, intended for the use of the Dauphin, Fénèlon's *Télémaque*, a Racine and a Corneille. All are printed in a transitional roman of a very light cut. The type had appeared already in 1782 in a prospectus of a book on the engravings of E. S. Bartoli (see Updike, fig. 162). Updike's figs. 163 and 164 show similar "maigre" romans, one of them being called a "gras", notwithstanding its extreme lightness. This last was used in a book printed by P. F. Didot le jeune, who had started a foundry in 1783. An edition of the works of Fénèlon, of which the first volume was printed in 1787 by F. A. Didot, is also set in a "maigre". But already in 1784 there had appeared another type cut in the foundry of F. A. Didot, a type which is of great importance in the history of roman. We reproduce a page from the "Avis" of an edition of Tasso's *Gerusalemme Liberata* (fig. 18), of which the first part is announced for June 1784. Following the definition of modern face given above, we must accept this type as a modern face and the first of its class. The thin, flat serifs, the verticality and abruptness of the shading (contrast the e of this type with that of any earlier roman) make this roman different only in degree of shading from the founts which Firmin Didot was later to cut. And yet the fact that the shading is not too exaggerated, together with the great skill of the engraver, make this roman of 1784 a far better type than the later designs which the Didots themselves came to prefer. In the same year F. A. Didot printed an octavo edition of *Télémaque* in a smaller size of the roman. Whether or not these two sizes were the work of Firmin Didot, by 1786 he had certainly produced two smaller sizes of the same design. These are found in the second edition of Pierre Didot's *Épître sur les progrès de l'imprimerie* (in this second edition the *Épître* follows his *Fables nouvelles*) and Pierre expressly states that the 8 pt. roman of the text and the 9 pt. of the "Avertissement", as well as the italic of the notes, were cut by his brother. The italic in which the first edition of 1784 was printed, he says, was cut a year ago, i.e. in 1783, by Firmin at the age of nineteen (he was born April 14, 1764). This italic had already been used in the books of 1783.

In the page reproduced from the prospectus of the Tasso it will be seen that attention is drawn to the paper on which the book is to be printed, *papier-vélin*, that is, wove paper, made by the Johannot of Annonay. In most of the Didot books of this period the use of *papier-vélin* is specially mentioned. There appear to have been three French firms who were manufacturing wove paper about this time, Réveillon at Courtalin and the Montgolfier at Vidalon, besides Johannot. Pierre Didot claimed to be the initiator in this matter, and he states his case in the notes to the *Épître*, where he admits that Baskerville had printed his Virgil of 1757 on wove paper. M. Marius Audin in his article, "De l'origine du papier-vélin" (*Gutenberg Jahrbuch*, 1928) has shown that the Montgolfier had a better claim to be the first French manufacturers. Whether Didot states the position with strict fairness is not our concern here, but it should be noticed that the use of wove paper gave a sharper impression, a result which was imperative with the delicately cut types which the Didots were introducing. Another technical development which served a similar purpose was an improved press, now being used by both Didot and by Anisson at the Imprimerie Royale. The notes to the *Épître*, which are full of

Le prix de l'exemplaire, composé de deux vo-
ımes in-4° sur papier-vélin de la fabrique de mes-
ieurs Matthieu Johannot pere et fils, d'Annonai,
remiers fabricants de cette sorte de papiers en
'rance, et orné de quarante et une planches y com-
ris le frontispice, sera de douze louis. Les sou-
cripteurs ne feront aucune avance, et ne paieront
u'à mesure qu'ils recevront la partie de l'ouvrage
chevée. Il sera partagé en quatre livraisons, com-
osées chacune de dix planches et de la partie du
exte correspondante.

La premiere livraison paroîtra dans le mois de
uin de cette année 1784; en la recevant on paiera
uatre louis. La seconde paroîtra dix mois après la
remiere, et alors on paiera quatre autres louis. Les
leux dernieres livraisons se feront de même de dix
n dix mois successivement; et l'on paiera deux
ouis pour chacune. Ainsi, à-peu-près à l'époque
ixée dans le premier prospectus, l'ouvrage sera
omplet; et l'on espere qu'il n'éprouvera plus de
etard.

Fig. 18. Didot's Modern Face, 1784

interest, include a relevant passage, in which Didot asserts that Anisson had copied the principle of the press introduced by his father, F. A. Didot. The note is appended to a passage about Baskerville, which reads: "Il n'y sut réformer un vice originaire Et n'en obtint jamais qu'un tirage inégal." The vice, says Didot, was due to the two pulls necessary with the old presses, in which the platen was only half the size of the forme, so that it had to be brought down twice for the printing of one sheet. There is an interesting passage on this "two pulls to the forme", in R. B. McKerrow's *An Introduction to Bibliography*, 1927, pp. 61–3 where the author dates the change to the larger platen at about 1800. The Didots were using such reformed presses by 1784, and claimed that a better impression was thereby obtained.

The Didot modern-face roman was again used in a Latin Bible of 1785 and in an edition of Bossuet's *Discours* of 1786. In 1788 the other branch of the family, P. F. Didot, produced an edition of the *De Imitatione Christi*, in new types by Henri Didot, son of P. F., which are almost modern face; in this fount the verticality of the shading is not completely carried out, as may be seen in the e. Again attention is drawn to the *papier-vélin*. But Firmin Didot was not content to stop here. His delight at his own skill in cutting fine hair-lines led him on to an over-modelling of his types, which became a European fashion and the hall-mark of what are called classical types. The continuation can be seen in the Lucan of 1795, described as being printed "typis P. Didot", though in fact they were cut by Firmin. Pierre Didot began a foundry of his own only in 1809. The full flower of the Didot modern face can be seen in the Virgil of 1798 and the famous Louvre editions (see fig. 19). These books won universal, or almost universal, praise, and as a result Firmin Didot in 1812 was invited to reform the typography of the Imprimerie Impériale. Pierre Didot himself started a foundry and with the help of Vibert, an engraver trained by Firmin, produced the series of modern-face types shown in his specimen of 1819. These he preferred to the Baskerville letters which he had purchased as a curiosity and which, as we shall see, he was anxious to dispose of. The Didot modern face remained the

Hancce ego editionem, novos et, confidenter
dicam, notorum hucusque omnium elegantis=
simos fratris mei Firmini Didot typos exhiben=
tem; puraque et candidiore charta, a consan=
guineo nostro Didot *d'Essone* feliciter con=
fecta, nitentem; simul et viginti tribus æneis
tabulis perite incisis, et ab egregiis pictoribus
Gerard et Girodet (qui proximos utriusque
magistro David honores in arte sua occupant)
delineatis, exornatam; ipse vigiliis curaque

Fig. 19. Didot's Modern Face, 1798

standard letter in France, and for the mass of books is still the normal design in use today. Although some French printers have joined in the revival of old face, the general typography has changed far less than in England. A glance at any dozen recent novels printed in France will show that the Didot tradition is by no means broken.

And yet there were protests even when Firmin Didot was at the height of his fame. In *The Fleuron*, no. 6, Updike gave a translation of a speech by one Citizen Sobry delivered in the year VII (1800) to the "Société libre des Sciences, Arts et Lettres de Paris", relating to the types of Gillé fils, a follower of Didot. Sobry declares that Garamond's types are more legible then Didot's, because Garamond emphasised those parts of the shape of his letters which distinguished them from one another, while Didot emphasised the parts which are common to all; cf., for instance, the u and n. He prefers the deep colour of Garamond to the grey of Didot, and declares that the Didots were led into error by copying the lettering of the engravers. According to Sobry, the last of the Anissons, who died in 1794 "révolutionnairement", always refused to adopt the Didot letter at the Imprimerie Nationale.

Anisson and Sobry were isolated cases, and most of the European typographers were seduced by Didot. The most famous of them, Giovanni Battista Bodoni of Parma, followed close in his footsteps. By 1787 he had cut types like the early Didot modern faces, used, for instance, for the Italian text of the *Lettre à M. le Marquis de Cubières*—the French text is set in a cursive, called by Bodoni "Cancellaresca"—and his name is especially associated with the fully developed modern face. This was because he was the most famous printer in Europe in his day, although as a designer of roman types he was never anything but an imitator of the French. His *Manuale Tipografico*, issued in 1818, after his death, is the most sumptuous display of modern-face types in existence. The book includes a long preface written by Bodoni from which great things might be expected. But it is disappointing reading. As to the design of types he has really very little to say, and part of what he does say is vague. He says that types owe their beauty in the main to four qualities: "regolarità", "nettezza e forbitura", "buon gusto" and "grazia". In Mr. H. V. Marrot's version of this preface published in 1925, these terms are translated "regularity", "smartness and neatness", "good taste" and "charm". By regularity Bodoni appears to mean the standardisation of those parts of letters which are the same. Smartness and neatness refer to technical qualities of clean casting. In the paragraph on good taste the writer talks mainly of simplicity, and as to charm he says that "letters have charm when they give the impression of being written not unwillingly or hastily, but painstakingly, as a labour of love". All this is rather vague and tells us nothing as to why Bodoni preferred the modern face and what he thought of contemporary typography, as compared with that of the fifteenth century.

In Germany, the Berlin type-founder, J. F. Unger, who is chiefly known for his light-faced Fraktur, received the sole agency for Didot types. A Sallust printed by him in 1790 is an example of his use of the Didot roman. In May of 1790, J. C. L. Prillwitz of Jena published his *Proben neuer Didotschen Lettern*, which led to disputes with Unger. Prillwitz's letters are so poor that Unger's objections might have seemed unnecessary. Brietkopf was also drawn into the discussion. The Leipzig founder seems to have been piqued because he had lost the chance of securing the agency.[1] Another German founder who imitated Didot and whose types are being used again today was J. E. Walbaum (Goslar, 1799, Weimar, 1803–36). Charles Enschedé's book shows examples of copies of Didot in Holland towards the end of the century. Anthony Bessemer, a Dutchman at work in Paris in 1795, supplied the Enschedé with a Cicero roman and italic, which are thoroughly modern face. In 1792 Hendrik van Staden had cut letters "naar de snee van Mr. Dido, à Paris".

The first English printer who modified the old-face roman in England was John Baskerville of Birmingham. He began work on his new types in 1750, and by 1754 had produced a specimen in the form of a prospectus of the forthcoming Virgil, which finally

[1] See Crous, *Die erste Probe Didotscher Lettern.*

appeared in 1757. Baskerville was well known on the Continent, and is generally said to have had much influence on Didot and Bodoni. But his influence seems to have been rather as a printer than as a designer of types. We have seen that his wove paper was copied in France, and his formula for book-production, his spaced capitals and leaded pages reappear in the books of the so-called classical printers. But in pure typography there seems to be no trace of a Baskerville school outside Great Britain, except of course in the use of actual Baskerville types. Didot proceeded from the "romains du roi", and would have so proceeded if Baskerville had never printed. Even in England, where there was a Baskerville period in typography, the modern face came from the French, and not as a development from Baskerville.

A comparison of the Baskerville and Caslon romans will show in what manner the former modified the old face. As a writing-master himself he brought the contemporary practice of calligraphers into typography. His types are rather more modelled and their shading rather more vertical than that of the Caslon letters. Contrast, for instance, the distribution of weight in the e (see fig. 20). As a result of the greater modelling the counters of the round letters are larger and the type as a whole is lighter. But the serifs are still inclined and bracketed, nor are the thin lines excessively thin; therefore the roman has in general much more the appearance of old face than of modern face. Of individual letters, the Q with its new tail and the curly-tailed R (in some sizes only) are conspicuous. In the lower case the tail of the g is not quite closed, and the w (upper case also) has no serif on the centre stroke. These are helpful as "spot" letters, especially the w in texts in English.

Baskerville died in 1775 and the fate of his stock has been a curious one. Straus and Dent (*John Baskerville*, 1904) give details of various printers at Birmingham and in the neighbourhood, including his own foreman, Robert Martin, who had strikes or matrices of the types. But the main stock was sold to Beaumarchais who intended to produce an edition of the works of Voltaire at his press at Kehl, near Strasbourg. A prospectus was issued in 1782 and the first volume appeared in 1784, the very year in which the

Didots produced the first modern face. The further history of the punches and matrices has been told by Mr. John Dreyfus in *The Survival of Baskerville's Punches*, Cambridge, 1949. Beaumarchais brought the stock back to Paris in 1790, set up a foundry and sold type to a number of French printers, including the Imprimerie Nationale. In 1818 Beaumarchais's daughters sold the material to

Caslon	*Baskerville*	*Modern-face*
m	m	m
e	e	e
g	g	g
r	r	r

Fig. 20. Specimen letters comparing the three types.

Pierre Didot. He apparently set no value on them and offered them to Francis Egerton, Earl of Bridgewater, in a letter here reproduced (see fig. 21).[1] The offer was not accepted and the stock descended through various Paris foundries, being occasionally used and described as "Elzevier ancien". Their true source was recognised by Bruce Rogers, who about 1920 bought some type for the Harvard University Press. The original punches and matrices have been acquired from Deberny and Peignot by the Cambridge University Press.

In spite of the fact that there was not sufficient enthusiasm for the Baskerville types to secure their preservation in England, yet the leading type-founders were paying him the compliment of

[1] The letter is in the British Museum and was reproduced by Robin Flower in *The Library*, 1909, pp. 151 *seq.*

imitating his designs. The early specimens of Isaac Moore of Bristol, the type-cutter to the Fry foundry, show romans which owe much to Baskerville. The distribution of weight and the modelling, as well as minor points like the tail of the g and the pointed apex of the A, are evidence of this fact, and in John Smith's *The Printer's Grammar*, 1787, where the Fry types are shown, the debt is admitted. In the Fry specimen of 1785 it is expressly stated in the preface that the types are modelled on those of William Caslon. But, in fact, this is only true of the smaller sizes, the larger being still the "Baskerville" types of Moore. Baskerville was dead and was not a competitor in the type-founding business. That the romans shown in Alexander Wilson's, the Glasgow founder's, specimen sheet of 1772 are derived from the same source, is generally admitted. William Martin, brother of Robert Martin, who worked with Baskerville, made some reputation towards the end of the century by the types which he cut for the Shakespeare Press, the favourite types of William Bulmer. These, too, are of the Baskerville school, as is particularly evident in the case of the italic. The excellent roman shown in Vincent Figgins's first specimen of 1793 is another example, and yet another is supplied by William Caslon III, after he had separated from the original Caslon firm and had bought the foundry of Joseph Jackson. His transitional roman appears in his specimen of 1798. The last quarter of the eighteenth century might well be described as the Baskerville period in English printing, both on account of the number of Baskerville designs which had been put on the market and because his formula for book-production had been widely adopted.

In 1788 John Bell, of the British Letter Foundry, issued his first specimen of type cut by Richard Austin. Attention was called to the important and beautiful Austin letters, still in the possession of Messrs. Stephenson, Blake & Co., by Mr. Stanley Morison in an article, "Towards an Ideal Italic", in *The Fleuron*, no. 5. Mr. Morison calls it "our first independent design", and further says: "while maintaining a predominantly old-face character (it) exhibits tendencies towards the modern face". Elsewhere, in his

Le 16 Janvier 1819.

My Lord,

J'ai fait depuis peu l'acquisition de tous les types de Baskerville, c'est à dire de tous ses poinçons en acier, et de toutes ses matrices de cuivre, en nombre d'environ vingt deux caractères différents depuis le plus petit jusqu'au plus gros romain et italique. C'est l'ensemble d'une des plus belles fonderies qui existent; et je l'ai acheté par occasion, et simplement comme objet de curiosité, n'ayant pas eu envie d'y mettre un grand prix, ma nouvelle fonderie à laquelle je travaille depuis huit années consécutives étant bientôt terminée. Cette fonderie de Baskerville se compose de plus de trois milles poinçons en acier, et d'autant de matrices. Beaumarchais la lui a payée vingt mille livres sterling. C'est de Madame Delarue, fille de Beaumarchais, que j'ai fait cette acquisition, partie en argent, partie en éditions imprimées par moi. Si, comme objet de curiosité, ce bel ensemble de types anglais parait vous convenir, j'ai l'honneur de vous le proposer pour le prix de six mille francs. De plus, dans quelque pays que ce fût, cette fonderie pouvroit encore faire un état à quelqu'un que vous auriez intention de récompenser, ou d'encourager.

J'ai l'honneur d'être avec respect, my Lord,
Votre très humble et obéissant serviteur.

P. Didot, l'ainé.

Fig. 21. Letter about Baskerville's types in Monotype Baskerville

John Bell, 1930, he has called it the first English modern face. It is significant that John Bell was in Paris in 1785, visiting the printers and type-founders. The only known copy of his specimen of 1788 is in the Bibliothèque Nationale in the Anisson collection. The type seems to be inspired by the Didot letter of 1784, which we have called the first modern face. There are a few reminiscences of Baskerville, for instance the Q, and some of the italic capitals, but these are minor points. Although reminding one of the early Didot, yet Austin's roman stops short of Didot in several important particulars. The serifs are flat (in the English size the serifs at the top of the ascenders are not quite flat, but they are in the larger size), but they are bracketed, and very delicately cut. The shading is not quite vertical, note the e, and is far from abrupt. The designer has supplied two K's and two R's, the curly-tailed and the earlier form, and two t's, the modern where the cross-stroke is not bracketed and the old form. He shows also a short-ranging J and modern figures. Mr. Morison seems to be justified in calling it an independent design, but according to our definition it should not be classed as a modern face, or, at any rate, not without limitation (see fig. 22). It may be added that the type was used occasionally by William Bulmer, as in Sir William Drummond's *Philosophical Sketches*, issued anonymously in 1795. The roman which Updike used for the text of his *Printing Types*, called "Oxford" and originally cut by Binney and Ronaldson of Philadelphia, seems to have some affinity with Austin's.

Austin under the pressure of fashion went on to cut several series of modern-face types, although during the years when the full modern face was becoming fashionable in England, he appears to have been engaged as an engraver of ornaments, the British Letter Foundry having failed in 1798. He cut modern types for the Wilson foundry at Glasgow and for William Miller at Edinburgh. By 1819 he had a foundry of his own in London, in Worship Street, called the Imperial Letter Foundry, and a specimen was issued in 1819. In the interesting introduction he says: "The modern or new-fashioned faced printing-type at present in use was introduced by the French, about 20 years ago; the old-shaped letters being capable of some improvement . . . but unfortunately for the typographic art, a transition was made from one extreme to the opposite: thus instead of having letters somewhat too

The modern or new fashioned faced printing type at present in use was introduced by the French, about twenty years ago, the old shaped letters being capable of some improvement...but unfortunately for the typographic art, a transition was made from one extreme to its opposite: thus instead of having letters somewhat too clumsy, we now have them with hair lines so extremely thin as to render it impossible for them to preserve their delicacy beyond a few applications of the lye-brush, or the most careful distribution; thus may types be said to be in a worn state ere they are well got to work. The hair lines being now below the surface of the main strokes of the letters, the Printer, in order to get an impression of all parts of the face, is obliged to use a softer backing, and additional pressure...In forcing the paper down to meet the depressed part of the face, it at the same time takes off the impression of part of the sides, as is evident from the ragged appearance of printing from such types.

Fig. 22. John Bell's Type, 1788

clumsy, we now have them with hair lines so extremely thin as to render it impossible for them to preserve their delicacy beyond a few applications of the lye-brush, or the most careful distribution; thus may types be said to be in a worn state ere they are well got to work. The hair lines being now below the surface of the main strokes of the letters, the Printer, in order to get an impression of all parts of the face, is obliged to use a softer backing, and additional pressure. . . . In forcing the paper down to meet the depressed part of the face, it at the same time takes off the impression of part of the sides, as is evident from the ragged appearance of printing from such types." He goes on to say that the types of thirty years ago were better, and further that the punches of the Imperial Letter Foundry will be cut in a peculiar manner, to assist this useful invention (stereotyping). What the peculiar manner is we are not told, but at any rate Austin seems to have avoided the evil results which he describes by slightly bracketing his serifs. His complaint against the modern face seems to be made on technical grounds, but at least we may draw the conclusion that he was not responsible for introducing the French new-fashioned faced types. His type of thirty years ago, the John Bell type, he would consider as belonging to an earlier and better period of letter-founding.

John Bell's newspaper, *The Oracle*, was printed in the early Austin type from 1792, and this fact seems to have influenced newspaper typography. The type was copied by Fry and later, in November 1799, *The Times* appeared in a new type from the Caslon foundry. In his article on newspaper types in *The Times Printing Supplement*, 1929, Mr. Morison shows this letter, which he describes as modern. It is like the Austin type in its bracketed serifs, gradual shading and not quite vertical colour. When compared with a type cut by Robert Thorne in 1800 the contrast is striking. In Thorne's letter we have an undoubted modern face, which so far as recorded appears to be the first to answer the definition of modern face which we have given. This letter of 1800 appeared in Thorne's specimen book of 1803, where all the letters described as new are modern face; another one is dated 1802 (see fig. 23). In the preface Thorne calls them "improved printing types". For some reason or other this new letter was highly popular and the other type-founders soon followed Thorne's example. Fry issued a specimen including some modern faces in the same year as Thorne, 1803;[1] these, together with the new letters of the Caslon firm, were shown in Stower's *Printer's Grammar*, 1808, where regret is expressed that Figgins's new letters were not yet ready. That the Fry Foundry was following the compulsion of

GREAT PRIMER, No. 1. NEW.

Quousque tandem abutere Catilina, patientia nostra? quamdiu nos etiam furor iste tuus eludet? quem ad finem sese effrenata jactabit audacia? nihilne te nocturnum præsidium palatii, nihil consensus bonorum omnium, nihil hic munitissimus habendi senatus locus, nihil horum ora vultusque moverunt? patere tua consilia non sentis? constrictam jam omnium horum conscientia teneri conjurationem tuam non vides? quid proxima, quid superiore nocte
ABCDEFGHIJKLMNOPQRST
UVWXYZÆŒ œ £1234567890
ABCDEFGHIJKLMNOPQRSTUVWXYZÆ

Fig. 23. Thorne's Modern Face

fashion rather than their own wish is evident from some words of Dr. Edmund Fry, the head of the firm, in the circular issued at the time of the sale of his foundry in 1828, quoted by Reed. After referring to the revolution in the type-founding trade, he says:

[1] William Savage, in his *Practical Hints on Decorative Printing*, shows a Caslon modern face and dates it 1796; but no such specimen appears in the Caslon specimen book of 1800.

"The Baskerville and Caslon imitations . . . were laid by for ever; and many thousand pounds worth of new letters in Founts . . . were taken from the shelves, and carried to the melting-pot to be recast into Types, no doubt in many instances more beautiful; but no instance has occurred in the attentive observation of the Proprietor of this Foundry where any Founts of book letters on the present system, have been found equal in service, or really so agreeable to the reader, as the true Caslon-shaped Elzevir types." It is a curious fact that the principal type-founders—the Caslons in their specimens of 1825 refer with regret to the original Caslon types no longer shown—and connoisseurs such as Hansard in his *Typographia*, are all agreed in condemning the new fashion, and yet all were forced to follow the taste of the day. Thorne appears to have enjoyed his success and went on to further exaggerations, to the cutting of fat-faced types, which in turn were imported into France. So far as the evidence of the type specimen books goes, Thorne appears to be the founder who was responsible for sponsoring the full modern face in England.

At this very time when the fate of English typography was being settled for the next century, there was a remarkable improvement in the standard of English book production, due to the work of Thomas Bewick as an illustrator, and of William Bulmer and Thomas Bensley as printers. Although they were clearly influenced by Didot and Bodoni, it so happens that the typography of their early and best period was not modern face. The type used by Bensley for printing Macklin's Bible and for Thomson's *Seasons*, 1798, was the earliest roman of Vincent Figgins, a transitional type, while William Bulmer's favourite roman, used in many well-known books issued by the Shakespeare Press, was that of William Martin. Martin was a brother of Robert Martin, who had worked with Baskerville, and his types show the influence of that designer, more particularly in the italic. The roman is definitely not a modern face, much less so than the John Bell type. It has the eighteenth-century R, ranging figures and a modern g with a curly ear, but the serifs are not quite flat and the stress not vertical. The g, which appears to lean backwards, is perhaps the easiest letter to recognise. No specimen seems to have been issued by Martin, but a specimen of a Liverpool printer, G. F. Harris, 1807, displays his types. Harris was successor to John MacCreery, who had used Martin's type in a poem entitled *The Press*, 1803.

CHAPTER FOUR

Roman

OLD-FACE TYPES IN THE VICTORIAN AGE

THE STORY OF the slow revolution in our book typography from the modern faces of the nineteenth century back to the old faces has not been recorded in much detail. One receives the impression that the Chiswick Press was an outstanding exception, and that the next event of importance in English typography was the founding of the Kelmscott Press. William Morris and his pupils certainly did much to raise the general level of printing, but as to the development of the book types used by the ordinary publishers they have nothing to do with the story. In 1840 our typography was without exception modern face. After that year the old faces crept in slowly, and their use gradually increased, year by year, until the picture is now reversed. This change-over would have taken place if Morris had never printed, and was in fact ensured before his first type was cut.

An account of the actual revival of Caslon Old Face by the young Charles Whittingham of the Chiswick Press may be read in the textbooks such as Updike. The reader may, however, be reminded that the story as there given is not quite complete. The printing of *Lady Willoughby's Diary*, in 1844, for Longmans, was not Whittingham's first experiment with the type. He had at the time several books in hand, to be set in Caslon, for William Pickering, and had already, from 1840, used Caslon capitals on title-pages for that enterprising publisher. The details are given in Sir Geoffrey Keynes's *Bibliography of William Pickering*. From 1844 the Chiswick Press frequently used the type. Of many successful volumes it is pleasant to recall that gayest of all school books, the Euclid of 1847, with its illustrations in colour.

At the Great Exhibition of 1851 Whittingham was one of the jurors for printing, and in his report, issued in 1852, he writes: "Mr. Whittingham at the suggestion of Mr. Pickering first reintroduced the old letters of Garamond and Jenson, and many of the London printers have since followed." The remark about the "many" London printers is somewhat surprising at that date, for it is only rarely that one comes across a book of the forties or early fifties set in an old face unless from the Cheswick Press. Whittingham's chief follower was a publisher and printer of religious books of the Anglo-Catholic school, Joseph Masters. In 1847 Masters had a book, *A Short Account of Organs*, printed in Caslon at the Chiswick Press. In 1848 he himself printed two books in the same style and type, a *Book of Common Prayer*, and J. E. Millard's *Historical Notices of the Office of Choristers*. The *Common Prayer* he describes as being printed in the "Old Elzevir type". A third volume followed in 1849, *The Devout Chorister*, by T. F. Smith. Amongst a large number of books in modern face Masters continued to produce an occasional volume in Caslon, all charming little books not unworthy of Whittingham. In the sixties the devotional books which he printed for the Rev. Orby Shipley are among his best work. By 1860 Caslon had become a favourite type for books of that class; for example, the *Pietas Privata*, 1859, was printed by J. Unwin for Ward & Co. in Caslon. A Catholic printer, John Philp, was yet another old face enthusiast. A page from his edition of the *Garden of the Soul*, 1860, is shown in Mr. Morison's *Four Centuries of Fine Printing*. Another of Philp's publications, also of 1860, was a music book, a *Cantata on the Passion of Jesus Christ*, of Saint Alphonsus Maria de Liguori, in which the title-page and preliminaries are handsomely set in Caslon.

Among early examples of Caslon-set books of a more general

nature are R. A. Willmot's *Pleasures of Literature*, published by T. Bosworth in 1852, and an edition of Tupper's *Proverbial Philosophy*, printed in 1854 by Vizetelly for T. Hatchard. The Tupper belongs to a group of books in old faces produced for Christmas and described in the advertisements as "Elegant Presentation Books". In 1855 Clay printed for Sampson, Low & Co., editions of Keats's *Eve of St. Agnes*, Thomas Campbell's *Pleasures of Hope* and Goldsmith's *Vicar of Wakefield*, all in old-face types. Similar volumes followed each year and a particular style of binding is associated with these books. They are all in embossed cloth covers, gaudily decorated. The advertisements in *The Publisher's Circular* become of interest on this point. This periodical was issued by Sampson, Low & Co., who no doubt were responsible for the new illustrated display pages, chiefly of Christmas books, set in Caslon capitals. The first occurrence of this new style was in 1854, although the books so advertised in that year were themselves printed in modern face. In 1855 there are half a dozen of these Caslon-set advertisements, three in 1856, none in 1857 and fifteen in 1858, most of the books being printed in old face.

The original Caslon was not the only eighteenth-century type to be revived. The example of the Chiswick Press had led other founders to look over their old stock, and we find, for example, Vincent Figgins in a specimen book of the fifties showing a page of the original romans of the first Vincent Figgins, dated 1795. Another transitional type of the end of the eighteenth century was used by the Brothers Dalziel, the wood engravers, who started their own "Camden Press" in 1857. This type, possibly a Caslon of the 1790's, may be seen in Doyle and Planché's *The Old Fairy Tale*, 1865. The roman can be distinguished from the original Caslon by the A, with a pointed apex, the Q with the tail starting inside the counter of the letter and the curly-tailed R. The italic has some unusual letters, the *b* and *p*, for instance, and is not really an old face at all.

The ordinary publishers as yet certainly did not believe that the old faces were more legible. They were all right for books which might or might not be read, but they were not going to use them for sensible reading matter. We may note in passing that Caslon was reintroduced into the United States in 1858, bought by L. Johnson & Co., of Philadelphia. The English founders were in no hurry to copy, and the next experiment was made by Whittingham himself.

This was the type known as Basle roman, which was cut for the Chiswick Press by William Howard of Great Queen Street. Updike, referring to its use by William Morris in 1889, says that it was cut about fifty years before that date. I have found no example of its use earlier than 1854, but possibly Whittingham's report of 1852, with its reference to the letters of Jenson, is an indication that it was in existence by that date. In 1854 it was used for the text of the Rev. William Calvert's volume of religious verse entitled *The Wife's Manual* (see fig. 24). There were later editions in 1856 and in 1861, both set in the same type. The title-page was set in Caslon, as there appears to have been only one size of the Basle roman, 10–11 pt., and no italic. William Howard was an ex-sailor, and from the account given of him in A. Warren's book on *The Charles Whittinghams*, 1896, seems to have been something of a character. He had a small foundry in Great Queen Street from 1842 to 1859 (he died in 1864), and was much employed by Whittingham. He had a hand in the cutting of the Chiswick replica of one of Caxton's types.

Apart from experiments to reproduce Caxton's books in type-facsimile, the Basle roman was unique in this country as an attempt to copy an early design. The type is based on the kind of roman used in the early part of the sixteenth century by Johann Froben, of Basle. It is a pre-Garamond roman, what we should call a Venetian rather than an old face, such as was in use at Basle and at Lyons, down to about 1550. It is a heavy face, with an oblique stroke to the eye of the e, and other characteristics which ally it with fifteenth-century types. The stress is definitely diagonal, so much so that the o has an angular appearance. The old-fashioned long s was used with the fount and the squarish terminals of this letter are conspicuous. The short s has a noticeably steep spine. An oblique stroke is used for the dot over the i, another fifteenth-century characteristic.

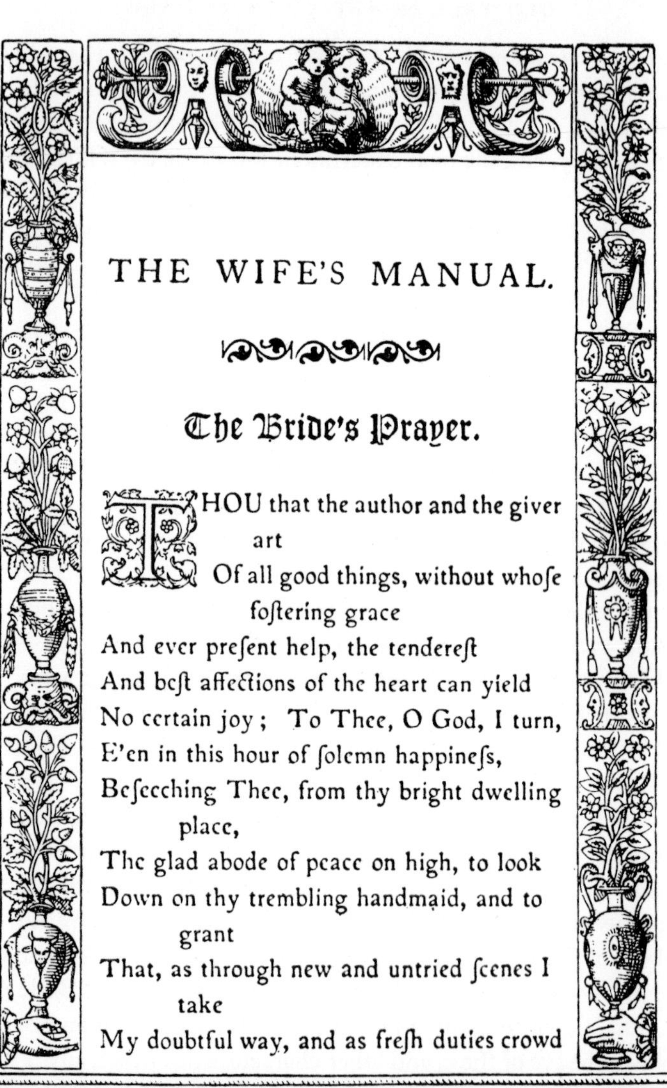

THE WIFE'S MANUAL.

The Bride's Prayer.

THOU that the author and the giver art
Of all good things, without whoſe foſtering grace
And ever preſent help, the tendereſt
And beſt affections of the heart can yield
No certain joy; To Thee, O God, I turn,
E'en in this hour of ſolemn happineſs,
Beſeeching Thee, from thy bright dwelling place,
The glad abode of peace on high, to look
Down on thy trembling handmaid, and to grant
That, as through new and untried ſcenes I take
My doubtful way, and as freſh duties crowd

B

Fig. 24. The Basle Roman

This type was much too exotic to appeal to printers in general, but its antique flavour attracted William Morris. In 1889 he had his prose romance, *A Tale of the House of the Wolfings*, set in Basle roman. He dropped the long s, but on the other hand he had his pages set solid—the pages of *The Wife's Manual* were leaded—which emphasised the blackness of the face. The title is in Caslon capitals, and the table of contents in an italic of earlier design. In another romance, *The Roots of the Mountains*, 1890 (the book actually appeared in 1889), Morris used the type again, but had a different e cut, one with the bar nearly, but not quite, horizontal. The only other books which I know of, set in Basle roman, are three volumes of religious verse by the Rev. Orby Shipley, *Lyra Eucharistica*, 1863; *Lyra Messianica*, 1864; and *Lyra Mystica*, 1865.

Many years after Whittingham had shown an interest in Caslon Old Face, in 1857, it made its first reappearance in a specimen book of the Caslon firm. In 1860 there appeared the first specimen of Miller & Richard's Old Style, a modernised old face. This was cut by their employee in Edinburgh, Alexander C. Phemister. In the specimen of 1860 eight sizes were shown, from great primer to pearl. The founders state that it was intended to meet the growing demand for old faces and explain that "they have endeavoured to avoid the objectionable peculiarities, whilst retaining the distinctive characteristics of the mediaeval letters". As to the word mediaeval in this connection, it is but one more example of the odd vocabulary used by founders. Old faces are certainly nearer in time to the Middle Ages than the modern faces, but to call the roman of the Italian Renaissance mediaeval is to make hay of typographic history. An examination of the type will reveal what the founders understood by the "objectionable peculiarities" of the earlier letters. It has two of the chief characteristics of the old faces, the bracketed and inclined serifs and the gradual stress.[1] On the other hand, the stress is vertical and there is a regularity and a certain sharpness of cut which are modern. The upper case is not unlike Caslon, but there is a uniformity of width about the letters which is

[1] This is not so in all versions of Old Style; for example, in Miller & Richard's No. 4 Old Style.

a relic of the modern face. For example, the H, M and W are narrower, and the bowls of the P and R wider than in Caslon. The A has a flat top (in Caslon it is oblique). The curves of the C and G are more open, and the C has no lower serif, while the top serif is more spur-shaped. In the lower case the bowl of the a and the eye of the e are larger, and the t is taller than in Caslon. These are no doubt the letters which appeared peculiar to type designers trained in the modern-face school. Perhaps the letter which differs most from Caslon is the g. The tail or loop begins with a steep inclination, a form which is possibly a reminiscence of the French Old Style or Elzevir, a type which just preceded Miller & Richard's design. However that may be, this g is a most useful "spot" letter. The italic is steeply but more regularly inclined than Caslon. Note especially among the capitals the A, V and W. In the lower-case there is one peculiarity that is easily remembered. The thin up-strokes take off from the very foot of the thick down-strokes. The main stem of the p is conspicuously tall.

This excellent face succeeded in certain quarters and found imitators before long. At least one may perhaps say "before long" on the subject of the slow-moving history of typography. Phemister, cutter of the original design, went to the U.S.A. in 1861, and by 1863 had produced for the Dickinson Foundry of Boston another version known as Franklin Old Style. He died in the United States in 1894, after a busy career as a designer of types. Genzsch & Heyse, of Hamburg, in 1868, showed their English Mediæval, for which they said they had procured matrices from a leading firm of English founders, presumably Miller & Richard. In the meantime in the *Printers' Register* for 1866 four interesting advertisements are to be seen side by side. Miller & Richard announced the completion of their series of Old Style types, while the Caslon firm assert that their Old Face is "invariably selected by the *Literati* as the only genuine Old Face Type". In September 1866 Stephenson, Blake & Co., of Sheffield, display their "New Series of Old Style Types", which differ in some small points from the original Old Style. The A has a pointed apex, the S a steeper spine, and the T spurs to its serifs. The angle of inclination of the italic is not so great. In October 1866 Reed & Fox, the Fann Street Foundry, show their "New Series of Mediaeval Founts", a close imitation of Miller & Richard; as to the name, if the original founders could refer to the old face as mediaeval, there is some excuse for Reed & Fox. In 1868 yet a third firm, the Patent Type-founding Company (afterwards Shanks), produced an Old Style.

It is evident then that by this time Old Style had been accepted and the fact can be illustrated from the printed books of the period. For example, John Payne Collier, one of the "literati" of the day, a well-known Shakespearian scholar, published privately many reprints of tracts from early English literature. From 1862 onwards these are generally printed in Old Style. An Edinburgh firm—it will be remembered that Miller & Richard's foundry was in Edinburgh—W. P. Nimmo, used the new letter from the early sixties. John Philp, from about 1867, seems to have preferred Old Style to Caslon, for instance, in his edition of Joannes Lanspergius's *An Epistle of Jesus Christ to the Faithful Soul*, 1867, and many of his later books. He was, however, no longer his own printer, but generally employed J. Ogden. About the same time, before 1870, Hodder & Stoughton also were issuing books of a religious nature in Old Style. Again the advertisements in the *Publishers' Circular* show that from 1864 Old Style began to rival Caslon in display.

On February 7, 1865, there appeared the first number of the *Pall Mall Gazette*, set in Old Style, a revolutionary change in newspaper typography. The example was followed by three other evening papers, *The Echo* in 1868, the *St. James's Gazette* in 1880, and later by the *Westminster Gazette*.

Herbert Horne's *Hobby Horse* of 1888 has often been quoted as the classical example of the use of Old Style and as a pioneer volume in the abandonment of the modern face. A trial number of the *Hobby Horse* had been printed in 1884, in Caslon, and the first regular issues from 1886 were set in a small size of Old Style. The larger size, used from 1888, certainly displayed the good qualities of the type, but by that date it had been used for more than twenty years and often effectively used. One printer in particular had not waited for the *Hobby Horse* to show the reading public what could be done with Old Style. This was Andrew White Tuer of the Leadenhall Press, a versatile printer and publisher whose work deserves to be better known.

Tuer (1838–1900) was born in Sunderland, educated at Newcastle upon Tyne and York, and came to London as a medical student at Guy's Hospital. He never completed his course there, and in 1862 we find him established as a wholesale stationer at 136 The Minories. In the following year he was joined by Robert Field, the firm being known as Field & Tuer. About 1868 they moved to 50 Leadenhall Street, where they printed and published *The Paper and Printing Trades Journal*, the first number of which is dated December 1872. This journal, one of the earliest of its kind, was published by Field & Tuer for nearly twenty years, being continued later by John Southward. From the first it was printed in Old Style with a display title, in the early numbers, in Old Style italic; after a few issues this titling was dropped and a block substituted. Some woodcut initials, generally reproductions from the sixteenth-century examples, were used as decoration. There is little or nothing of lasting interest in the matter of the periodical, and the advertisements are not above the average of the day, that is to say they are very poor. Even Field & Tuer's own advertisements of their Japanese papers and their "Stickphast" are no exception.

The most interesting part of Tuer's career begins in 1879 when his firm began to publish books, including a number of which Tuer himself was the author or compiler. His first book was an odd publication called *Luxurious Bathing*, in which a treatise on baths from a hygienic point of view was combined with twelve landscape etchings by Sutton Sharpe. The typography of the book was Caslon Old Face. Several other editions appeared with etchings from other hands, equally disconnected from the subject of Tuer's essay. The firm continued to publish down to Tuer's death in 1900, at first as Field & Tuer; in the course of the year 1890 Field's name dropped out and the imprint became the Leadenhall Press. Field, who died in 1891, appears to have been merely a sleeping partner or financial backer. The publishing house could boast of a fairly extensive and somewhat unusual list. A number of their books dealt with the fashions and manners of bygone days, many were reprints of earlier books illustrated by contemporary blocks, and others reprints of early children's books. Among the authors on their list were Max O'Rell (Paul Blouet) and Jerome K. Jerome. A few of the books were printed in Caslon and a few in an old face which is not Caslon, but the great majority in Old Style. Only rarely did the Leadenhall Press think it desirable to use a modern face; one example is a lecture by Sir William Flinders Petrie printed in 1884. A few of the firm's earlier efforts might be described as "arty"; but Tuer's taste seemed to improve rapidly and the failures were few. The books were well printed, on good paper, with interesting title-pages, and decorated often with a daring quite exceptional at the time.

The most important of Tuer's own works was his life of the engraver, Bartolozzi, which appeared in two large volumes in 1882; there was a smaller edition without the plates in 1885. The text is set in Old Style, the title in a bold italic of the old-face school, and the running title in Old Style italic within rules. The title-page is well arranged and very full. Tuer never shrank from saying all that he wanted to say on the title-page and would not have approved of the anaemic fashion of the present day. The imprint is set in swash capitals, one of Tuer's failings; he was altogether too fond of these letters and his more usual imprint in lower case Old Style italic is much to be preferred. The Bartolozzi is a large quarto, the size of the page being controlled by the plates, and Tuer is very successful with the help of ruled pages, in coping with the difficulties of a large page. Another volume on an ambitious scale is Hoppner's *Bygone Beauties*, ten portraits engraved by Charles Wilkins about 1803 and printed from the original plates. The title-page shows a daring mixture of types; one line is in a large lower case old face, one in Lyons capitals, one in outline capitals, and others in italic. The text pages are decorated with head and tail pieces and woodcut initials.

Tuer's best volume is perhaps *The Follies and Fashions of our*

Grandfathers, published in 1886. The title is set in an outline italic, the chapter headings in outline roman capitals, and the text in Old Style. Some unusual small script initials are used at paragraph openings. The text consists of extracts from fashion and other journals of the year 1807, bearing on social life, with illustrations, printed, many of them, from contemporary plates. Tuer contrived to get hold of an extraordinary number of old copper-plates and made very good use of them. In an article in no. 6 of *The Fleuron* Mr. Morison noted Tuer's use of outline letters, and said that he was the only printer between Thorne and our own generation who used such letters. The roman capitals are possibly the Caslon outline capitals dating from about 1790; the italic outline letters may have been prepared at the Leadenhall Press by cutting away the centre of the strokes. Tuer was of an ingenious turn of mind, and the use of the script initials we have mentioned was another of his tricks. The smaller ones are simply the capitals of a fount of English ronde, and the larger the capitals of one of the fancy types of the age, resembling the Caslon Gutenberg series. As detached thus by Tuer from their proper founts they are not unsatisfactory.

Before Tuer's career came to an end, Caslon Old Face and Old Style had ceased to be exceptional in our typography. Yet so conservative are English printers that there was no demand for any further experiments either in the reproduction of early designs or in types of any originality. In the United States Franklin Old Style was soon followed by Ronaldson and a number of types of the same school. It is a striking fact that in this country, apart from the privately owned faces of the Kelmscott, Doves and other presses, the first acceptable book type to be cut after the Old Style of 1860 was the "Monotype" Imprint of 1913. In view of this conservatism it is perhaps not so surprising to find that today more books are actually set in Old Style than in any other type. But these are no longer the choicest books. Old Style has become the poor relation in typographical society. It is left for the cheapest kind of books, often ill-used, impressed on the wrong sort of paper, and seldom given a chance to show its best qualities. It has had its day, and in its day has played a role of some importance.

A parallel movement in France begins with the work of a printer of Lyons, Louis Perrin. Having to print a work by Alphonse de Boissieux on ancient inscriptions found in Lyons, Perrin cut a special series of capitals based on the inscriptional lettering. These were widely copied and were introduced into England by the Chiswick Press under the name of Lyons capitals. They were shown in a specimen of 1867, and, as we have already seen, were often used by Tuer. Like another famous inscriptional alphabet, the lettering of the Trajan Column at Rome, the Lyons capitals are of varying width, letters like E and M being narrower than the round letters D and O. In the modern face this sound principle of letter designing had been ignored and capitals had become of uniform width. Perrin afterwards cut a lower case for these capitals and called the fount "Caractères augustaux". In 1857 a Parisian founder, Théophile Beaudoire, followed Perrin with his type known as Elzevir, of which the upper case closely resembled the Lyons capitals and of which the lower case should more properly have been called Garamond. However, Elzevir had become the established name for French Old Style and it is Beaudoire's type which seems to have been known to Phemister, if we may judge by the similarity of the lower-case g's. In spite of these Elzevir types and the work of publishers like Jules Claye, the Didot influence has remained stronger in France than the corresponding modern face in England. The majority of French books are still set in "Didot".

CHAPTER FIVE

Italic

THE OLD FACE

ITALIC IS NOW a subdivision of roman; it bears the same relation to roman which Schwabacher bears to Textura. It is a cursive letter and was so called by its original designers, "corsiva" or "cancellaresca", and is still called *cursiv* by the Germans. Our name, italic, which we get like roman through the French, is not good, since roman is equally an Italian letter. Italics may be divided into four main groups: (*a*) the Aldine, (*b*) the Vicentino group, (*c*) the group which is the contemporary of old-face roman, and (*d*) the modernised italics. The Aldine letter had a comparatively short career, and is historically perhaps of less importance than the Vicentino group.

The Aldine italic (see fig. 25) was based on the hand employed in the Papal Chancery for the inditing of briefs, as opposed to the more formal Bulls, which were written in a gothic script, the "lettera da bolle". The Chancery cursive goes back to the early years of the fifteenth century. A reproduction of a brief written in this letter is given in Steffens's *Lateinische Palaeographie*. Aldus adopted it because it made possible the printing of much matter in a small space and not because of any beauty in the design. On the score of beauty this mean letter ranks considerably below the italics of our second group. Nor did Aldus improve the appearance of his type by the large number of tied letters which he used. The engraver employed by Aldus for the cutting of this cursive and apparently of all his types was one Francesco Griffo of Bologna. This fact is established by three contemporary documents. Aldus himself in the preliminaries of the Virgil of 1501, the first book in which the new letter was used,[1] writes: "In grammatoglyptae laudem. Qui graiis dedit Aldus, en latinis Dat nunc grammata sculpta daedaleis Francisci manibus Bononiensis." Geronimo Soncino, a well-known printer of Hebrew, used a second italic, cut by Griffo, at Fano in 1503. In the dedication of the Petrarch printed in that year, Soncino says: "... ma anchora vn nobillisimo sculptore de littere latine, graece, et hebraice, chiamato M. Francesco da Bologna, l'ingeno delquale certamente credo che in tal exercitio non troue vnaltro equale. Perche non solo le vsitate stampe perfectemente sa fare: ma etiam ha excogitato vna noua forma de littera dicta cursiua, o vero cancellaresca, de la quale non Aldo Romano, ne altri che astutamente hanno tentato de le altrui penne adornarse, ma esso M. Francesco è stato primo inuentore e designtore, el quale e tucte le forme de littere che mai habbia stampato dicto Aldo ha intagliato, e la praesente forma, con tanta gratia e venustate, quanta facilmente in essa se comprende." This passage confirms Aldus, although Soncino thought that the printer had taken some of the credit due to the type-cutter, and gives us the correct name of the letter. Finally Griffo himself began to print small editions in a third italic of his design at Bologna in 1516. In the preliminaries to his Petrarch he says: "(hauendo pria li greci e latini Carattheri ad Aldo Manutio R. Fabricato, de li quali Egli non sole in grandissime richezze e peruenuto, ma nome immortale appresso la posterità se uendicato) Ho excogitato di

[1] On the title-page of the Letters of St. Catharine of Siena, 1500, there are four words set in the new type. In *Philobiblon*, Hft. 10, 1933, there is reproduced an Italian poem in four columns, headed "Frotola noua". The poem is set in a roman type first used by Aldus in 1499, and a few letters, some l's, e's and r's, are italic. T. de Marinis who describes the sheet, which is in a private library, considers that this is probably the first appearance of italic. But the poem is not necessarily printed by Aldus. The type is a common one, nor do we know of anything else of the kind from the Aldine Press. Even if it were printed by Aldus, the date, 1499, is a mere assumption.

nouo cotal cursiua forma qual extimo a qualunche rudita persona essere per piacere. . . ." Whether his grievance against Aldus was well-founded or not, does not concern us here. At any rate these documents are evidence that Francesco indeed made history in typography. We have discussed the importance of the Aldine roman, and the lasting fame of the Aldine Greek and its notorious effects on Greek typography is a well-known story. The immediate

IVNII IVVENALIS AQVINA
TIS SATYRA PRIMA.

S EMPER EGO AVDITOR
tantum? nunquám ne reponam
V exatus toties rauci Theseide
Codri?
I mpune ergo mihi recitauerit ille
togatas?
H ic elegos? impune diem consumpserit ingens
T elephus? aut summi plena iam margine libri
S criptus, et in tergo nec dum finitus, Orestes?
N ota magis nulli domus est sua, quam mihi lucus
M artis, et æoliis uicinum rupibus antrum
V ulcani. Quid agant uenti, quas torqueat umbras
A eacus, unde alius furtiuæ deuehat aurum
P elliculæ, quantas iaculetur Monychus ornos,
F rontonis platani, conuulsaq; marmora clamant
S emper, et assiduo ruptæ lectore columnæ.
E xpectes eadem a summo, minimóq; poeta.
E t nos ergo manum ferulæ subduximus, et nos
C onsilium dedimus Syllæ, priuatus ut altum
D ormiret. stulta est clementia, cum tot ubique
V atibus occurras, perituræ parcere chartæ.
C ur tamen hoc libeat potius decurrere campo,
P er quem magnus equos Auruncæ flexit alumnus,
S i uacat, et placidi rationem admittitis, edam.
C um tener uxorem ducat spado, Meuia thuscum
F igat aprum, et nuda teneat uenabula mamma,
P atricios omnes opibus cum prouocat unus,

Fig. 25. Aldine Italic

reputation of Francesco's italic was considerable, as we shall see, but in this case not so enduring. An attempt was made in 1858 by Sir Anthony Panizzi to identify Francesco with Francesco Raibolini, the painter, also of Bologna. The argument was demolished by Giacomo Manzoni in his *Studii di bibliografia analitica*, and the matter clinched by the publication by Adamo Rossi[1] in 1883 of a document from which it appeared that Francesco's family name was Griffo.[2] However, the identification with Raibolini was still repeated by English writers. The legend that Griffo's italic was modelled on Petrarch's hand is equally persistent. In the Aldine Petrarch of 1501 it is stated that the *text* of the poems was based on the manuscript in Petrarch's hand, then in the possession of Pietro, afterwards Cardinal Bembo, and now preserved in the Vatican Library. A misunderstanding of this passage probably explains the legend. Aldus's words are: "Aldo a gli lettori . . . hauendoui una volta detto cheegli è tolto dallo scritto di mano medesima del Poeta hauuto da M. Piero Bembo." The statement is repeated in the colophon of the book. One Lorenzo da Pavia, an agent of Isabella Gongaza, the Duchess of Mantua, refers to this copy in Petrarch's hand in a letter of July 26, 1501. He writes: "E se a avuto el Petrarcha proprio de man del Petrarcha coscrito de sua mano eo lo avuto in mane ancora io. Et e de uno padovano che la stima asai si che lano stampato a letera per letera como questo con molta diligencia."[3] This, of course, has no reference to the type, but to the text. Griffo returned to Bologna in 1516 and printed a few small volumes in 32mo in his third italic. His career ended in disaster in 1518. Documents were discovered and published by Emilio Orioli[4] in 1899, from which we learn that in

[1] In the *Atti della r. deput. di storia patria per le provincie di Romagna*, 1883, p. 412.

[2] G. I. Arneudo in his *Dizionario Esegetico*, 1917–24, art. Francesco da Bologna, claims to have seen a document which shows that his family name was *Giusto*, and not *Griffo*, but states that he cannot trace his reference.

[3] See A. Baschet, *Aldo Manuzio*, 1872, p. 113.

[4] See *Atti e mem. della r. deput. di storia patria per le prov. di Romagna*, Ser. III, vol. XVII, p. 162 *seq*.

May 1518 Francesco during a quarrel with his son-in-law seized an iron bar and inflicted such wounds as led to the death of the younger man. From the documents it does not appear whether Francesco was hanged for this crime, but merely that he was no longer living a year later.

Griffo's first italic was immediately copied, the chief plagiarist being the Lyons printers, Balthazar da Gabiano and Barthélemy Trot. The privilege which Aldus obtained from the city of Venice was of no avail, even in Italy. The Giunta in Florence copied him in 1503, and in 1506 Benedetto Dolcibelli was printing at Carpi in another version of the Aldine letter. The Lyons printers made use of Aldus himself to correct their editions. Balthazar da Gabiano was the representative in Lyons of a Venetian company, "La Compagnie d'Ivry". Aldus in his protest of 1503 says of the Lyons counterfeits that they were printed on inferior paper, "graveoleus", and that the consonants were not joined to the vowels. He pointed out misprints, for example in the Virgil, and when Gabiano reprinted the Virgil he corrected these errors; but other errors crept in, e.g. *stulus* for *stultus* on the first page. In 1512 Barthélemy Trot joined Gabiano, and it was he who introduced the fleur-de-lis found on many of these Lyons copies.[1] In Italy, in the first half of the century, the majority of printers had their Aldine italic. We may cite three well-known editions as examples of the popularity of the letter, the *Decameron*, printed in 1516 by Filippo Giunta at Florence, the first editions of Macchiavelli's works printed at Rome by Antonio Blado in 1531 and 1532, and Marcolini's Dante of 1544. These types depart from the original chiefly by cutting down the enormous number of ligatures at first used by Aldus. The design remains the same and the model is adhered to in the consistent use of upright capitals. In the italic of Paganino and Alessandro de Paganinis, used at Toscolano from about 1520, the lower case also is more upright. The Paganinis had two sizes of this type, and used a roman a, as well as the usual one-storeyed a. The original chancery hand was sloping, but as we shall see in some

[1] See *Impressions de Louis Perrin*, Lyons, 1923. Introduction by Marius Audin.

later examples, cursiveness rather than inclination seems to be the essential characteristic.

The earliest italic used at Paris, by Guillaume Lerouge, was again all but upright, more particularly the largest of the three sizes, with which the printer used a gothic upper case. The second Paris imitation of the Aldine letter was that of Thielman Kerver, with which, an unusual experiment, he printed a Book of Hours in 1517. In the colophon of this edition the printer says: "sub hoc recenti sculpture stilo nup'rime efformate". Pierre Gromors had an italic by 1520 (see G. Fichetus, *Consolatio luctus & mortis Parrhesiensis*), and in 1523 Pierre Vidoue began to use a fount acquired from Basle (see the edition of Erasmus, *De interdicto esu carnium*). Coyecque, in the *Bulletin de l'histoire de Paris*, 1894, pp. 149, 150, cites a document according to which Wechel sold to one Hennequin de Breda "deux lettres façon d'Allemaigne, dont l'une gregue et l'autre d'itallicque", a document dated May 28, 1528. "Allemaigne" here most probably means Basle. Sebastien Gryphius of Lyons, on the other hand, who obtained most of his types from Basle, appears to have bought in Italy the italic used in the *Opere Toscane* of Luigi Alamanni, 1532, and the *Opuscula aliquot* of Cardinal Bembo, also of 1532. Alamanni, an exile at the court of King Francis I, received a payment of 1,500 livres on November 30, 1513, in order to purchase types in Venice.[1] This type, however, is not Gryphius's usual italic. That was an Aldine, probably acquired in Basle, and used in the same way as the original Aldine, for the printing of classical texts of considerable length. Gryphius sold his books in Spain with such success that this style of chancery came to be known to the Spanish writing-masters as *Grifo*. Robert Estienne at Paris also used Aldine italic for similar classical texts, for example an edition of Cicero's *Letters to Atticus* of 1543 in small octavo and an even smaller edition in 1547 in sextodecimo.

Estienne's italics may have been cut by Claude Garamond, who certainly cut two sizes for his own use after the Aldine model. In

[1] Cimber and Danjou, *Archives curieuses de l'histoire de France*, Ser. I, vol. III, p. 85.

1545 Garamond became a publisher along with Pierre Gaultier and Jean Barbé. He gives an account of the venture in the dedicatory epistle to the first book published, the *Pia et religiosa meditatio* of David Chambellan. He there says: "Tum vero foelicter me rem aggressurum si quam proxime fieri posset, Italicam Aldi Manutii literam, novis exprimerem caracteribus . . . Italicarum itaque proxime ad Adlinos literarum typos sculpo, quam foelicter alii judicabunt."[1] He cut two sizes, a Glossa, which is the type used in the Chambellan and in the four other books bearing Garamond's name in the imprint, a Thucydides, a Diodorus, a Lactantius, and a Juvencus, and a larger size, which Mrs. Warde finds on one page of the Juvencus.[2] The sole particular in which Garamond's design departs from the Aldine is in the capitals, which are inclined; but even here the fount is equipped with upright capitals as well, and the inclined upper case appears on the title-pages and headings only. We shall see that the fashion of sloping capitals had been introduced some years before.

The new letter was introduced into Germany by an obscure printer at Erfurt, Sebald Striblitza, and was used for the text of an edition of Columella in 1510, *De cultu hortorum*. Three other books from his press are known, all set in italic: Platina's *Dyalogus contra amores*, Papinius Statius's *Achilleis*, both 1510, and an undated edition of Ulrich von Hutten's *Nemo*. The type measures 91 mm. for 20 lines. The upper case is modest in height, has heavy slab serifs and an unusual R; in the lower case the conspicuous letter is an upright g. It is a copy of the Aldine, but a less close copy than many later founts.

The statement that Johann Froben of Basle used italic in 1513 in his edition of Erasmus's *Adagia* has been often repeated, starting probably from a slip in Stockmeyer and Reber's *Beiträge zur Basler Buchdruckergeschichte*, 1840. There is no italic in that edition, though Froben's Aldine Greek appears there for the first time. His italic is not found until 1519. The Basle example was quickly

[1] A full translation of this epistle was given in *The Fleuron*, no. 3, pp. 49, 51.

[2] See her article in *The Fleuron*, no. 5, p. 138.

taken up, and by 1520 four other German printers had acquired the letter, Knoblouch and Schott at Strasbourg, Schöffer at Mainz, and Johann Soter at Cologne. Proctor says that Knoblouch's type is like Schöffer's, and Schott's like Froben's. On the printer's specimen of Johann Petri of Nuremberg, 1525, two sizes of italic are shown which are again very like Froben's, so like that possibly the matrices came from Froben. Several references will be made below to types acquired from Basle and all the evidence seems to point to that city as an important centre of type-founding during the second quarter of the sixteenth century. Other German printers who had the Froben italic before 1530 were Nicolas Schmidt (1522) and Valentin Schumann (1527) at Leipzig, Sigmund Ryff (1523) at Augsburg, and W. Köpfel (1526) at Strasbourg. Peypus at Nuremberg had the same italic as Petri. In the Netherlands Thierry Martens at Louvain seems to have been the first printer to introduce the Froben letter in 1522.

In England the earliest italic is that of De Worde, in two sizes, used in 1528 in Wakefield's *Oratio de laudibus trium linguarum.*[1] A more interesting cursive is that of Thomas Berthelet in which in 1530 he printed a Vatican decree on the matrimonial affairs of Henry VIII, *Acta Curiae Romanae in causa matrimoniali cum Catharina Regina*. These italics were certainly imported; De Worde's type is found at Antwerp; Berthelet's was used at Cologne by E. Cervicorn from 1525, by Wolfgang Köpfel at Strasbourg, and by Guillaume Morrhé at Paris.[2]

Besides the chancery hand from which these Aldine italics were derived there was also a more formal variety, of which a magnificent example was shown by Mr. Morison in *The Fleuron* (no. 6, p. 97) from a sixteenth-century manuscript written for Cardinal Grimani, a commentary on St. Paul's Epistle. This "cancellaresca formata" was the hand practised by the writing-masters of the sixteenth century, and was by them translated into type more than twenty years after the date of Griffo's first cursive. The first writing-master who printed specimens of his hands was Lodovico degli

[1] See Isaac, *op. cit.*, vol. 1, fig. 10b.

[2] On these types, see *The Library*, June 1936, pp. 70–82.

Arrighi da Vicenza, a "scrittore de' brevi apostolici", as he describes himself in his book of 1522. This professional calligrapher had apparently been in Rome for at least a dozen years before the publication of this book. In 1510 he was part publisher of a book of travels, the *Itinerario de Ludouico de Varthema Bolognese nello Egypto*, printed by Stephano Guillireti.[1] The first part of Vicentino's writing book of 1522 is printed entirely from wood blocks, but the second part, *Il modo di temperare le penne*, printed at Venice about 1525, has a page of text printed from type. In 1524 Vicentino began printing at Rome and issued a few small books in his new italic. In the imprint of these books his name is coupled with that of another printer, Lautitius Perusinus, styled in one of the books "Intagliatore". Vicentino's partner was probably identical with the Lautizio de Bartolomeo dei Rotelli commended by Benvenuto Cellini as an engraver of seals. It may be presumed that he was the actual cutter of the type. The books printed in this cursive were chiefly the works of contemporary men of letters, short poems or speeches, and not voluminous texts like the Aldine series. Vicentino's press was a small one, and his purpose was to issue a few select books in a beautiful setting. The cursive which he designed was a formal letter based on the hand which he himself practised; the letters are narrow, but separately formed and with a slight inclination. The ascenders are given rounded terminals in the place of serifs. The capitals are upright, but are varied by the introduction of swash letters. Nineteen small books printed in this cursive in the years 1524 and 1525 are known.[2] In the following year Lautizio's name has disappeared and a new cursive is used. This is still a formal chancery, but with serifs in place of the rounded terminals, and without the swashes. It is of about the same size as the earlier type (about 16 pt.), but of a larger face. It is noteworthy that almost all the italics of the Vicentino group have generous ascenders and descenders, and seldom measure less than about 16 pt. Economy of space was not considered in their design. Only six books printed by Arrighi in this type has been recorded,

[1] See *The Fleuron*, no. 7, p. 167.
[2] See the list below, pp. 130, 131 and fig. 26.

I RITRATTI
DI.M.GIOVAN GIωRGIO
TRISSINO.

ITROVANDOSI Messer Lucio Pompilio in Ferrara, et in casa di Madωnna Margarita Cantelma Illustre Duchessa di Sωra, ne la quale v'εra una brigata di valorose dωnne, ε di accostumatissimi Giovani, da le preghiere di tutti constretto, così a parlare incominciω. Se io hω bεne la intentione vωstra inteso Gratiosissima, et Illustre Madωnna, ε parimente quella di tutta questa nobilissima compagnia, voi volete, che per me vi si narrino quelli ragionamenti, che furono tra Messer Piεro Bembo, ε Messer Vicεntio Macro fatti in Milano; de i quali conciω sia cωsa che voi n'habbiate udito ragionare da chi nε nomi, nε luωghi, nε tεmpi vi seppe ordinatamente distinguere, hωra da me, come da persona, che presεnte vi fue, questo partitamente ne ricercate; et io lo farω piu chε volentieri; perciω che, havendoli altre vωlte ridetti, parmi assai bene

A y

Fig. 26. Vicentino's Italic

the last being an edition of the Latin poems of Hieronymus Vida issued in May 1527. The mercenary armies which sacked Rome so thoroughly in that year entered the city on May 6. As Vicentino's name does not occur again in any recorded book or document, it is possible that he met his death, as did many other citizens, in that catastrophe. We shall see that his types had considerable influence among his contemporaries, and not only his types, but his style of book-production also. He avoided all ornamentation, and except for two small initials found in one of his books, the *Oratio de pace* of Pope Julius II, 1526, had no decorative woodcut material, not even a device. In several particulars he affected the manuscript style; his books had only a half-title, and blanks were left to be filled in by the illuminators. The copy of the Hieronymus Vida, 1527, in the British Museum, printed on vellum, has been so illuminated. Many of Vicentino's imitators followed the severity of his style when using their formal chancery types, and even in a small point like the use of a diamond-shaped full-stop, recalled his practice. But after the first generation Vicentino seems to have been forgotten, to be rediscovered in the nineteenth century by Giacomo Manzoni. However, Manzoni's account of him in his *Studii di bibliografia analitica*, 1881, is concerned with the calligrapher and very little with the printer. The interest of our generation in Vicentino, exemplified by the re-cutting of his types, is due to Mr. Stanley Morison.[1]

The sixteenth century was the age of italics, especially in Italy where they were first designed, and in that country between 1500 and 1600 possibly as many books were set in italic as in roman. While the italics of the first quarter of the century were Aldine, those of the second were quite as often copies of Vicentino's letters. Among the men of letters who chose Vicentino as their printer was Gian Giorgio Trissino, the author of the tragedy, *Sofonisba*, and of an epic poem, *Italia liberata dai Gothi*. In 1524 Trissino had five books, including the *Sophonisba*, printed in Vicentino's fount with the calligraphic ascenders. Some extra

[1] See his reproduction of Vicentino's writing books, the Pegasus Press, 1926.

Greek letters were introduced in order to carry out Trissino's theories on Italian orthography, and for the first time a distinction was made between medial u and v. In one of the books or tracts, an *Epistola* dealing with the introduction of these new letters, the author pays a tribute to Vicentino, declaring that he has surpassed all the men of his age not only as a calligrapher, but also as a designer of types. Trissino in 1529 employed Tolomeo Janicolo of Brescia to reprint his works in his native town of Vicenza. A copy of Vicentino's type was used for these reprints and also for Trissino's translation of Dante's *De vulgari eloquentia*. These beautiful books, printed in folio and decorated by a handsome device of Jason's Golden Fleece—apparently Trissino's device, but adopted by his printer—have made Janicolo's name well known to bibliographers. Janicolo issued a specimen of his type, one of the earliest and least known of such advertisements, on which he makes no mention of Vicentino.[1] One other Italian printer imitated this cursive of Vicentino, F. Minitius Calvus at Milan. This Calvus had been a printer at Rome in Vicentino's lifetime, and was still there in 1531. In 1540 he printed at Milan *Torricella, Dialogo di Otho Lupano*, in his cursive, making great use of swash capitals. Of about the same year is an undated piece concerning Pietro Aretino, *Abattimento poetico del divino Aretino*. About half a dozen books are recorded printed in this type by Calvo and his successor, Andrea Calvo. Another Milanese printer, Giovanni Antonio Castellione, used a handsome cursive, akin to Vicentino's in several particulars; it has the same swash capitals, calligraphic ascenders and g, but it is upright. The Grimani manuscript, referred to above, is written in an upright chancery, and the writing book of Ferdinando Ruano, *Sette Alphabeti*, Rome, 1554, shows the construction of an upright "cancellaresca formata". Cursiveness and not inclination is the characteristic of chancery, but generations of printers have been so accustomed to the inclined italic that they have come to believe that the word means sloping. Castellione used his handsome letter in 1541 in the *Gallorum Insubrum Antiquae Sedes* of Bonaventura Castillioneus. Another

[1] A copy as in the British Museum.

humanist interested in the Gallic antiquities of Lombardy, Gaudentius Merula, used the same italic at a private press at Borgo Lavezzaro, near Novara, in 1542. Another fine book in the same letter is H. Girava's *Dos libros de cosmographia*, Milan, 1556 (cf. fig. 27).

Vicentino's later type, that used in 1526 and 1527, proved to be the forerunner of an even larger group of formal cursives. It came

IN dextra lapidis elaboratiſſimi Aquila viſitur
trunco Inſidens. Quæ in roſtro auis pennam tenet:
ad Leuam altera Aquila ſphæræ ſupereminet ſerpentem
mordicus tenens. Quid ſuper hac ſculptura cõſultus An-
dreas Alciatus Gaudentio Merulæ reſcripſerit; accipe;
Quòd petis(inquit) à me Hieroglypha illa tibi explicem
quæ à Nicolao Caſtellioneo accepiſti; vix auſim ego quic-
quam ſcribere; ne quod dicitur; noctuas Athenas. Adde

Fig. 27. Upright Chancery Italic

into the possession of Antonio Blado, the greatest printer at Rome in the sixteenth century. Blado's edition of Sannazaro's *Sonetti* of 1530 is perhaps his earliest book printed in this fount, and was followed by many others. The brothers Dorici, contemporaries of Blado, had a similar type, in which they printed the book of Ferdinando Ruano, already mentioned.

But it was at Venice that the influence of the Blado italic is chiefly to be traced. Vicentino's writing book was followed in 1524 by the similar work of a Venetian master, Giovantonio Tagliente. His book includes a number of pages printed from type, a cursive resembling Vicentino's later type but with rather more inclination. Tagliente's type is found both in the many editions of his calligraphic book and also in some of his other, mathematical works. The brothers Nicolini da Sabbio, who printed for Tagliente, had an italic in the same style as the Blado, which appears in most of the books from this busy press. A good example may be seen in the preliminaries of Greek books which they printed at Verona, e.g. the Epistles, 1529, and the Acts of the Apostles, 1532. Another distinguished Venetian printer, Francesco Marcolini da Forlì, printed mainly in italic, and his use of cursive founts illustrates the fashion of the day. He had at least seven founts in italic. The two smallest sizes (about 10 pt. and 9 pt.) were used for notes only, and may be described as Aldine. Two others, used in the last years of his career, from 1556, were of foreign origin, one from Basle and one French. We refer to these again below. No. 5 was the Aldine used in the Dante, but even with this, besides the usual lower-case g, Marcolini had the second g with the calligraphic tail. The remaining two italics are of the Vicentino school, and it is these that were used for the text of most of his books. The larger type, again of about 16 pt., is akin to the Blado, swash capitals are used, the calligraphic g, and a ligature gg, the large ampersand &, and the diamond-shaped full-stop. *Il Petrarcha Spirituale*, 1536, and several books of Pietro Aretino are printed in this italic. Later, Marcolini spoilt the fount by using a thick-faced upper case, a strange mistake for such a printer to make (cf. the *Prose di Bembo*, 1538). The smaller type is even more remarkable, as in it the principles of the formal chancery are applied to a letter of the Aldine size. All the characteristics of the larger italic just described are found, and the essential difference between the two schools is clearly illustrated. The letters are separately and carefully formed, and in consequence the appearance of a hasty script which typifies the Aldine is avoided. An edition of Petrarch's Sonnets of 1539 is set in this type, and later, in 1551, a volume of letters addressed to Aretino. Aretino was interested in good typography, and in his earlier days at Rome had had some books printed by Vicentino. He was intimately associated with Marcolini, who in fact had published five of his books even before he became a printer. In the first ten years of his career Marcolini printed at least twenty-five books by Aretino. In one of them, the *Ragionamento de le Corti*, 1538, there is a reference to a new type of Marcolini's, which from the date must be the italic of Petrarch's Sonnets. One of the characters in the *Ragionamento* says: "Io volevo vedere quella lettera cosi bella, che egli ha fatto gitare di nuovo."

The first German printers to copy the Vicentino cursive were the Viennese printers, Hieronymus Vietor and Johann Singrenius. In Gollob's *Der Wiener Holzschnitt*, 1926, there is a reproduction of the title-page of the *Periochae omnium librorum Veteris Instrumenti*, Singrenius, 1531. The title is set in a calligraphic cursive with long descenders without serifs, and an unusual ligatured ct. It is perhaps nearer to Tagliente's italic of 1524 than any of Vicentino's, and so faithfully represents the Italian cancellaresca, that it might almost be classed as a script type. Already in 1530 Vietor had used the type in Gennadius, *De synceritate Christianae fidei*. The cursive was used also at Cracow by Vietor, who in 1531 set the whole text of a Latin version of a speech of Demosthenes, the *De Pace*, in this unusual type.[1]

We have already referred to the few italics which were in use at Paris up to about 1525. Apart from the books of Guillaume Lerouge the volumes set in italic were few in number. It was Simon de Colines who first made the new letter popular in Paris, and he copied both the Italian schools. For his small editions of the Latin classics dating from 1533 he used an Aldine italic. A larger type, first used in Paulus Cerratus's *De Virginitate*, 1528, with its swash capitals, ampersand &, calligraphic ascenders and lowercase g, can have had no other source than the Vicentino letter (see fig. 28). Colines's third and largest italic, used in 1536 for the text of Diego de Sangredo's *Raison d'architecture*, has the same characteristics except that he has now gone back to serifs, just as Vicentino did in his later type. Books from Colines's press are numerous—some 800 are recorded by Philippe Renouard—and examples of all his italics are readily found. Whether he himself was a punch-cutter or whether he employed Claude Garamond, is not known, but we may at any rate reject the assumption of Auguste Bernard that these italics were cut by Geofroy Tory, who used no cursive founts at all in his own press. Colines died in 1546

[1] See a reproduction in *The Fleuron*, no. 7, p. 148.

and by that date French punch-cutters had made important alterations in the design of italics. But in the meantime one other Paris printer had followed Colines's lead. Robert Estienne had for the most part kept to the Aldine tradition, for his books were of a similar character to those of Aldus, namely, editions of classical texts of considerable length. But one of his books is manifestly in the Vicentino style, an edition of an Italian classic, Luigi

Nuenta ſecuit primus qui naue profundum,
i Et rudibus remis ſollicitauit aquas:
Qui dubijs auſus committere flatibus alnum:
Quas natura negat, præbuit arte vias.
T ranquillis primum trepidus ſe credidit vndis:
Littora ſecuro tramite ſumma legens.
M ox longos tentare ſinus, & linquere terras,
Et leni cœpit pandere vela noto.
A ſt vbi paulatim præceps audacia creuit:
C ordáq; languentem dedidicere metum:
I am vagus irrupit pelago: cælúmq; ſecutus,
Ægeas hyemes Ioniúmq; domat.

Fig. 28. Colines's Italic

Alamanni's *La Coltivazione*, 1546. The type closely resembles Colines' third italic, and the absence of decoration, blanks being left for initials, together with the absence of any subsidiary type, even on the title-page, further connect this book with the methods of Vicentino, Blado and Marcolini.

One would hardly expect to find an example of a Vicentino italic in an English law book of the sixteenth century, yet oddly enough the best example of the school outside Italy and France turns up in the *Registrum brevium* printed by William Rastell, London, 1531. The title is set in Textura, but the whole of the text in a calligraphic italic with swash capitals, probably copied from Colines. The punches may have been cut in Antwerp, as the type is found there in the *Oratio pro Pauperibus* of Christianus Cellarius printed by Hendrik Peetersen van Middelburch, in November

1530. In England the type is found for occasional use in a number of books, and with various printers, but in one other book only as a main body type, as in the *Registrum brevium*, i.e. in Robert Recorde's *The Pathway to Knowledge*, R. Wolfe, 1550. A little of it is found in other books from Rastell's press, and more in the only book known to have been printed by William Baldwin, *The Canticles or Balades of Salomon*, 1549, in which the title and text of the songs are set in the fount.[1] It travelled to Ireland and appears on the title-page of the first book printed in Dublin, a *Common Prayer*, by Humphrey Powell. Another of these Vicentino types is one used by Peter Perna (1522–82), an Italian Protestant exiled from Lucca for his religious opinions. About 1560 he printed at Basle several books of another Italian Protestant exile, Bernardino Ochino. These books, some with Perna's imprint and some without, are set wholly or in part in a cursive reminiscent of Vicentino. Although he uses the Aldine ampersand, his fount has a number of the Vicentino details, calligraphic ascenders, swash capitals, etc.

The latest member of the Vicentino group which I have found appeared at Amsterdam in 1613 in Hondius's edition of Mercator's *Atlas*. In the preliminaries of that edition some passages are printed in a cursive not unlike the Blado, and with all the usual characteristics of this group, calligraphic g, large ampersand, etc. Some of the ascenders are calligraphic and some have serifs; the upper case is inclined. It is not a good type of its class, but its use in 1613 along with a Granjon italic and another contemporary Dutch italic brings out the contrasting points of the two schools. The type occurs again in the *Atlas* of 1619, and in other books, printed by the younger Hondius, Henricus, e.g. in Robert Hues's *Tractatus de globis*, 1624. Jodocus Hondius, the father, who died in 1612, was Mercator's son-in-law, and had acquired Mercator's stock. It may be remembered that one of the earliest works of this famous map-maker was a writing book printed at Antwerp in 1540, which is devoted entirely to the Italian hand. This was the hand used by Mercator for the lettering of his maps, and again by Hondius, who also

[1] Cf. Isaac, *op. cit.*, vol. II, fig. 6*a*.

engraved a writing book, the *Theatrum artis scribendi*, published about 1595. Last of all the younger Hondius produced the italic of 1613, which has many resemblances to Mercator's lettering. As Henricus was born only in 1597, it may be presumed that Jodocus designed the new type, on the model of his own Latin script as shown in his *Theatrum* of 1595.

The logical step of fitting an inclined italic with an upper case at the same angle was not attempted by the original designers of cursive. The first printer to make the experiment seems to have been Johann Singrenius of Vienna. In Gollob's *Der Wiener Holzschnitt*, 1926, p. 73, there is a reproduction of the title-page of the *Vita Eremitae a Diuo Hieronymo conscripta*, 1524, showing the earliest use I have seen of this italic.[1] The type was used also by Nicolas Schmidt (Faber) at Leipzig in Schedel's *Nouus hortulus anime*, 1527, and in a Psalter of 1533. The undated edition of Melanchthon's *Elementa puerilia*, where the title is set in this italic, may be the work of a third printer. This new type is not especially attractive and seems to have been little used, but the problem of inclining the capitals was attacked with fair success; the inclination is, at any rate, more uniform than was achieved in the second type of this class.

The second italic with an inclined upper case can be traced to Basle, and will be referred to as the Basle italic. This is a remarkable letter in design and remarkable in its popularity, which endured for some twenty years. The earliest recorded book set in this italic came from the press of Sebastien Gryphius of Lyons, the *Epigrammata* of Claudius Rosselettus, dated 1537. Gryphius used the type as much as anyone, but appears to have obtained it, like many of his other types, from Basle. In 1538 there was issued an edition in Greek of the works of Galen in five folio volumes. Five Basle printers were concerned in the publishing and printing of this edition, Cratander, Hervagius, Isengrin, Bebelius and J. E. Froben. The privilege from Francis I is dated December 20, 1536. Evidently the work was in hand some time before 1538. The preface of 13 pages by the editor Gemusaeus, dated March 1, 1538,

[1] For another reproduction, see *The Fleuron*, no. 7, p. 146.

and a further preface in vol. v, are set in our italic. The device on each title-page was formerly used by Thomas Wolff, who had been the official printer of the city of Basle. Michael Isengrin, who printed vol. v of the Galen, used the type in other books of the same year, 1538, e.g. Aristotle, *Opera*, and Solinus, *Polyhistor*. (See fig. 29.)

The lower case of the Basle italic is a large letter of considerable slope, while the upper case is an extraordinary collection of letters at all angles. The M, N, R and V are the strangest. The O and Q are upright, and the A and P are swash letters. The designer can never have meant these capitals to stand in line together, and yet many contemporary printers did make the attempt. All the designers of old-face italics appear to have found a difficulty in giving a consistent slope to the upper case. In spite of the odd capitals the type has character, and certainly contemporary printers approved of it. No italic of the day is found in the hands of so many different printers. Apart from Basle, where it is particularly common, all the leading printers of Lyons had it. Christian Egenolff at Frankfurt, W. Rihel at Strasbourg, Ponce Lepreux at Paris, and Reinier Wolf and Richard Grafton in London, were among its admirers. Updike, who shows a page of the type (fig. 104), remarks on its widespread use in Venice. Giovanni Griffio, Giolito and Marcolini among other printers at Venice used it for preliminaries, and sometimes even a whole book was set in it, e.g. Xenophon's *Guerre dei Greci*, 1550. In other Italian cities it is found at Florence, at the Giunta press, at Rome with the Dorici, at Bologna, Mantua, Padua and Rimini.

In Basle there was also a smaller size of the type (about 11 pt.) in fairly common use, but this size was little favoured in other countries. The widow of Ulrich Morhard used it from 1556 at Tübingen. Richard Grafton in London also had this size.[1]

The Basle italic may be taken as inaugurating the old-face group, and the next step is the establishing of this style by French type-cutters, and in particular by Robert Granjon. There are a number of contemporary references to the dealings of Granjon with various printers, but nowhere any explicit attribution to him

[1] See Isaac, *op. cit.*, vol. II, fig. 33*b*.

of the earliest French old-face italics. By old-face italic we mean the kind of letter of a marked inclination in both upper case and lower case which was usual in European typography from about 1540 down to the time of Caslon. It is the italic which accompanies the old-face roman, although it originated somewhat later and

10 LIBER

Cui licet accedat Virtus, tamen uſquè priores
Fert Fatum parteis in re quacunque gerenda.
Fato Romani poſt tot diſcrimina, poſt tot — omanorum Im-
Prælia, debellatum Orbem rexere monarchæ: — rium ut creuit.
Roma caputq; fuit Mundi, priùs exiguus grex
Quam paſtorum habitabat, & errans exul ab aruis
Finitimis (ut aſylum) poſt ſcelus omne colebat.
Mox Fato inclinante, ſuis ſpoliata triumphis — deinde corruit.
Corruit, & patrio (infandum) iugulata tyranno
Nil, niſi nomen, habet Romæ, deſertaq; ſordet.
Fato etiam Græci nil non potuere uel armis, — ecorum poten-
Vel ſtudiis: terra omni poſthabita, auxit Athenas

Fig. 29. Basle Italic

was not at first designed as a companion letter. Like the Italian cursives, these French italics were cut and used as independent letters. As to their origin such evidence as we have points to Robert Granjon as the designer of the earliest and most popular of them. Granjon was the son of a Paris printer, Jean Granjon, and is first heard of in 1545,[1] when he rented a shop "aux Grands Joncs". From a document of August 9, 1546, it appears that Granjon was

[1] See Renouard, *Imprimeurs Parisiens*, revised edition in the *Revue des Bibliothèques*, 1925.

in the habit of visiting Lyons every year.[1] In 1557 he settled in Lyons and married Antoinette, daughter of Bernard Salomon, the artist who illustrated the books of Jean de Tournes. From a document of August 24, 1547,[2] we learn that one Gaspard de Molina ordered from Granjon types St. Augustin and Nonpareille like those supplied to Tournes and Gryphius, "diverses espèces de caractères, S. Augustin, Nonpareilles . . . ainsi que ledict Granjon les a baillées par cy devant à Jehan de Tournes et à Griffius". If we can identify these types the document becomes important. Nothing is known of Molina, who may have been only an agent, but the press of Jean de Tournes had not been long established at this date, and the number of his types was still small. As to the Nonpareille, Tournes does not appear to have used so small a size (about 6 pt.) by 1547. But of St. Augustines, the only type which can be in question is the italic used in the *Recueil des Œuvres* of Bonaventure des Periers, 1544, in *Les Marguerites des Marguerites*, 1547, and in many other of his early books. The same type is found in the books of Gryphius, for example on the title-page of the Horace of 1545. Gryphius did not use it much, as it was too large a letter for the kind of book which he normally printed, namely classical texts. Moreover, the type was used at Paris, e.g. by L. Grandin in Demosthenes' *Oratio contra Philippi epistolam*, 1543, by Denis Janot in the *Recueil de vraye poesie Francoyse*, 1544, and by Michel de Vascosan in a Ronsard of 1549. When Granjon himself began to print at Paris in partnership with Michel Fezandat in 1549, he used a very similar italic; cf., for example, *Le Tombeau de Marguerite de Valois*, and Cardano's *De subtilitate*, 1550 (see fig. 30). Tournes's type has an inclined upper case, as had all subsequent italics. The A is a swash letter of the same design as the A in the Basle italic. Tournes used this type as a letter of some elegance suitable for volumes of verse. In the preface to his Petrarch of 1545 he refers to his purchasing of new types for such a purpose, "havend' io fatto tagliar questi caratteri (i.e. those used in the

[1] See Coyecque, *Recueil d'actes notariés relatifs à l'histoire de Paris*, tom. II, no. 4170.

[2] See Baudrier *Bibliographie Lyonnaise*, vol. I, art. Molina.

ILLVSTRISS. ET EX-
cellentiſsimo Ferrando Gonzaghæ,
Principi Malfetæ, Arrianiq; Duci,
domino Vaſtallæ, prouinciæ Inſu-
brũ, & Cæſaris exercituũ Præfecto,
Hiero. Cardanus medicus Mediola.
S P D.

OMnes fermè gentes ætate no ſtra, Princeps Illuſtriſsime, Deum venerantur: ſed tamen nulli quod optimum factu eſt, id optima ratione efficiunt, niſi ſoli ſapientes. Quidam enim Deum ob id adorant, quòd eum colendo multa ſperant bona, ſpernando bona magna mala timent: itaque non hîc amor eſt, non veneratio, ſed potius ſpes, aut metus. Et quanquam hic metus aut ſpes non fruſtrà eſſent (quæ certè inania ſunt, ſi ad mortaliũ euentus, non ad animæ præmia referantur) nihilominus optimi facti cauſſa nõ optima eſſet. Nũc autẽ (vt opinor) hæc non ſolùm recta nõ eſt, ſed etiam vana in illis cultus diuini ratio. Sunt alii, qui ex conſuetudine propria, aut aliorum, Deum venerantur: atque vt hi prorſus nulla laude digni ſunt, ita illi qui ob legum metum ſolum

Aa ii

Fig. 30. Granjon's St. Augustine, Paris, 1547

Petrarch, a smaller size) et altri propri per stampar poeti, e altri opere da piacere". In 1549 Fezandat printed by himself *Le Temple de chasteté* of François Habert in a new italic, a beautiful letter with remarkably small, inclined capitals, and a conspicuous lower-case v. A few years later this same letter was used for the text of a number of Jean de Tournes's books, both prose and verse. Perhaps the best-known is the edition of the *Œuvres* of Louise de Labé, 1555. When we find that these two italics were used at Paris before they appeared in the books of Tournes or any other Lyons printer, we may infer that the types were cut in Paris. It is hardly likely that a Paris printer of that date would have applied to a Lyons type-founder for his material. With the support of the De Molina document and the knowledge of the connection between Fezandat and Granjon, we may conclude that the designer was Granjon.

Other italics of Tournes have been attributed to Granjon, the fount for instance in which the verses of the *Metamorphose figurée*, 1556, is printed, which Updike describes as silvery. A larger italic, a "Gros Texte", used in the Virgil in the French version of Louis des Masures, 1560, and in several books of the poet and mathematician, Pontus de Tyard, e.g. the *Solitaire Second*, 1555, has one characteristic which is common to other admitted italics of Granjon, that is the use of extra sorts with a prolonged final stroke intended for the filling up of a line. This "Gros Texte" of Tournes has swash capitals, but inclined, the G being a reversed H. Tournes used the type first in 1549, and in the same year it is found at the press of the De Marnefs at Poitiers, in Macault's version of Cicero's *Philippics*. The family of De Marnef also printed at Paris, and we should expect them to deal with a Paris rather than a Lyons founder.

The admitted italics of Granjon are those shown on the Egenolff-Berner sheet of 1592, already referred to for its romans. Seven sizes of italic are assigned to Granjon. The largest, a Parangon, has an e with a prolonged tail. This closely resembles the largest italic of Tournes, used only in preliminaries, for example, in Jacques Bassantin's *Discours astronomique*, 1557. Again we may compare

EPITOME ROMANAE HISTOriæ Dionis Nicæi de vigintiquinque principibus Romanis, & à Pompeio Magno, vsque ad Alexandrum Mamææ filium, Ioanne Xiphilino authore, & Gulielmo Blanco Albiensi interprete.

È DIONIS LIBRO XXXV.

VM Consules sortirentur, Hortensio, ut bellum gereret cum Cretensibus, obuenit. Sed is vrbe delectatus, & foro, in quo primum locum post Ciceronem obtinebat, collegæ vltrò exercitum cessit, ipse in vrbe remansit. Metellus autem in Cretam missus, totam insulam cepit: deinde etsi impediebatur à Pompeio Magno, qui per id tempus habebat totius maris imperium, & continentis, quæ non abesset à mari longiùs itinere trium dierum, tanquam insulæ ad ipsum quoque spectarent, tamen eo inuito bellum Cretense confecit, de quo triumphauit, & Creticus cognominatus est. Iisdem temporibus L. *Lucullus, cum Mithridatem, Tigranémque Armenium, reges Asiæ bello superasset, & terga vertere coegisset, Tigranocerta obsidebat. Sed eum grauibus incommodis affecere barbari, non solùm coniectis telis, sed etiam naphtha, quam tor-*

Hortensius vrbe magis quàm bello delectatus.
Metellus in Cretam missus.

L. Luculli In Asia res gestæ.
L. Lucullus.

a 5

Fig. 31. Granjon's Cicero Italic

the italic of the preliminaries of Plantin's Polyglott Bible, 1570, which is almost certainly Granjon's. In Max Rooses' *Le Musée Plantin* there are many references to dealings between Plantin and Granjon, who for a time, in the years 1565 and 1566, was living in Antwerp. In the period 1560–70 he has been called by Max Rooses, Plantin's "principal fournisseur". In 1563 Plantin drew up an inventory of his stock, and among the matrices mentioned are "le Bréviaire italique de Granjon, le Grec de Granjon, l'italique supérieure de Granjon, une autre italique de Granjon, une troisième italique de Granjon, le texte romain de Granjon, la Parangonne italique de Granjon, le Petit-Canon romain de Granjon, une italique nommée L'Immortelle de Granjon, une lettre française de Granjon". This list includes 10 founts supplied by Granjon by 1563, of which 6 are italics, 2 roman, 1 Greek and 1 "civilité". From 1565 to 1570, when the recorded dealings between the two cease, Plantin acquired or ordered about 15 other Granjon founts. On January 16, 1565, Granjon furnished 4 founts of Hebrew; on February 3 Plantin orders a fount of "gros grec à la faceon de celuy du roy de France accordant sur le Parangon"; on July 5 there is an agreement for a supply of two italics, one of "Garamont" size, and the other "Philosophie". In 1566 Plantin receives punches of "Garamonde Petit Romain" and of "Médian romain", also punches of fleurons, numerals, capitals and types of music. On September 7, 1566, there is an agreement for a supply of civilité. At this date Granjon was living in Antwerp. In January 1567 Granjon receives payment for another civilité. In April Plantin receives matrices of a Parangonne cursive, and an Augustin italique; in May he orders punches and matrices of a petit canon romain. In November 1569 Granjon supplies punches and matrices of Syriac for the Polyglott Bible. The last record is of April 18, 1570, when Plantin orders the punches and matrices of an italic Grande-Ascendonica. The Cicero italic of Granjon shown on the Egenolff Berner sheet appears in Plantin's *Index*, 1567, on C4. It is found at Lyons from 1554 (see fig. 31).

From the books printed by Plantin we know that he had a large and interesting series of italic types. Some of these we can connect

auoir esté deffaits par leurs princes, et l'auons veu de nostre temps: mais que les peuples ayent esté destruits par leur Roy, nous ne l'auons iamais veu, ny ouy dire.

On recita au Duc Galeace, qu'il y auoit dans Milan vn aduocat subtil à trouuer le moyen de faire les causes longues, et les procès immortelz, quand il l'auoit entrepris par faueur ou par argent. Le Duc le voulant experimenter, s'enquit à vn sien mel d'hostel s'il estoit rien deu à ceux qui le fournissoyent de marchandise. Fut trouué le boulenger à qui on deuoit cent liures: au nom duquel il se feit adiourner pour comparoir deuant le Senat. Et s'estant adressé à cest aduocat, luy demanda conseil pour delayer le payement. L'aduocat luy promit de trouuer les moyens et cautelles, que le boulenger ne toucheroit deniers d'vn an, voire de deux s'il vouloit. La cause actionée et presté à iuger, le Duc demanda à l'aduocat, s'il estoit

esser stati disfatti per i loro principi, e lo hauemo veduto del nostro tempo. Ma che i popoli sianno stati distrutti per il Re loro, noi non lo hauemo giamai veduto, ne vdito dire.

Fu recitato al Duca Galeazzo, che dentro a Milano v'era vno auocato suttile a ritrouare il modo di fare le lite luongue, e i processi immortali, quando l'haueua per impresa, per fauore, o per dinari. Il Duca volendolo isperimentare, fece inquisitione al suo maestro di casa, se v'era nessuno debito a quelli che lo forniuano di mercantie. Fu truouato il Bolongiere à cui cento lire erano debite: in nome del quale egli si fece acitare per comparere dinanzi al Senato. E indrissatosi a questo Auocadore, gli domandò consiglio per indugiare il pagamẽto. L'Auocato gli promisse di truouar i modi e cautele, che il Bolongiere non toccarebbe dinari d'un anno, anzi ne de duoi. se egli voleua. La lite fornita, e presta a giudicare, il Duca domandò

Fig. 32. Granjon's Civilité and Immortelle

with Granjon, and others, too, have an historical interest. Plantin's first italic, that in which the majority of his early books are printed (note that italic is still widely used for the main text), is about 11 to 12 pt., in modern measurements, or 20 lines measure 80 mm.; the fount has narrow and tall capitals. It was used by other Antwerp printers (first 1553), in Germany and by John Day in London.[1] *Les Secrets de Alexis Piemontois*, 1557, shows three italics; the main text is set in a St. Augustin which seems to be identical with the type used by Tournes, which we have attributed to Granjon. In Plantin's *Index Characterum*, 1567,[2] this italic is shown on C3. There are two larger italics in the introductory matter; the first measures 117 mm. for 20 lines. This type is not connected with Granjon but is of particular interest for its use by English printers. A good example may be seen in James Peele's *The manner and fourme how to kepe a perfecte reconyng*, R. Grafton, 1553, and in Cuningham's *Cosmographical Glasse*, John Day, 1559. Other London printers had it even earlier (cf. Isaac, *English Types, 1503–58*, the 111 italic). To us it seems to be a characteristic English italic because of its frequent occurrence. The third italic in the *Alexis* is a Gros Parangon (20 lines=143 mm.). This appears in the *Index Characterum* on B4, and is assigned to the founder, François Guyot.[3] This type too was commonly used in England, by John Day, for instance (cf. fig. 257 in Updike). It is one of the types formerly supposed to have been cut by Day. In another Plantin book, the *De regni institutione* of Foxius Morzillius, 1557, we find a type of much the same size as that used by Grafton, a Gros Texte, but this time an italic in common use in Paris, for instance, with Chrestien Wechel as early as 1547. In 1558 in *Les Épîtres de Phalaris* we meet a smaller italic, a Cicero, with a conspicuous initial v, which we have found used by Tournes at Lyons in the *Louise de Labé* and other works, and which we have assigned to

[1] Also at Emden. See Isaac, "Egidius van der Erve", in *The Library*, December 1931.

[2] A reproduction of the unique copy in the Plantin Museum was issued by Douglas McMurtrie, 1924.

[3] Cf. Reed, new edition, pp. 92, 93, and H. Carter, *op. cit.*, in *The Library*, September 1956.

Granjon. In 1564 we find yet another Gros Texte, a type shown on C2 of the *Index Characterum* and on the Egenolff-Berner sheet of 1592 as a Granjon. The "Immortelle de Granjon", an interesting italic, again with a conspicuous initial v, which we know from

EX PHILOSTRATI

IMAGINIBVS FA-
BVLAE.

FABVLAE ſe ad Aeſopum, ſua in eum beneuolen-
tia cõferunt, quod ſatagat ſui: fabula quippe & Ho
mero & Heſiodo, nec non & Archilocho in Lycamben
curæ fuit. ſed ab Aeſopo humana omnia ad fabellas re-
dacta ſunt, ſermone brutis non temerè impertito. nam
& cupiditatem imminuit, & libidinem inſectatur, &
fraudem. Atque hæc ei leo quiſpiam agit, & vulpes, &
per Iouem equus, nec teſtudo muta, ex quibus pueri di-
ſcunt, quæ in vita gerantur. Habitæ igitur in precio fa-
bulæ, per Aeſopum accedunt ad ſapientis ianuam vittis
eum deuinctura, coronaq́; oleagina coronaturæ. hic, vt
puto, fabulam aliquam texit. riſus enim faciei, & ocu-
li in terram defixi id præ ſe ferunt. pictorem, fabula-
rum curas remiſsiore animo indigere, non latuit. Philo-
ſophatur autem pictura & fabularum corpora. Bruta
enim cum hominibus conferens, cœtum circa Aeſopum
ſtatuit, ex illius ſcena confictum. Chori dux vulpes de-
picta eſt. vtitur enim ea Aeſopus miniſtra argu-
mentorum plurium, ceu Dauo
Comœdia.

AESOPI

Fig. 33. Granjon's Cicero Currens

the Egenolff sheet, I have not found in Plantin's books, although it was, as we have seen, included in Plantin's list of his stock in 1563. This "Immortelle" is found in London used by John Day, among others (see the reproduction in Isaac's article, *The Library*, September 1933, fig. 23. See also fig. 32.)

There is still one more Granjon italic, the *Littera Currens Ciceroniana* shown in one long line on the Egenolff sheet and appearing on C4 (lower half) of the *Index Characterum*, 1567, which is perhaps the most interesting of all. In a Plantin book there is a good specimen in the *Emblemata* of Sambucus, 1566. In the *Index* the specimen shown begins with the word *Philosophia* and *Philosophie* was also a name for this size of type. Now in July 1565 Plantin ordered from Granjon the punches and matrices of a Philosophie, and it seems likely that this is the type in question. The type appears in many places even before its appearance on the Egenolff sheet. In 1565 Sir Thomas More's *Opera* was printed at Louvain by P. Zangrerus in this italic. In 1566 Feyerabend of Frankfurt had an Æsop printed in the same type (see fig. 33). In the same year Peter Perna of Basle was using it, the Heirs of Steelsius of Antwerp in 1568 and Birckmann at Cologne in 1569. Later we find it used by the Elzeviers of Leyden (see L. van Aitzema, *Historia pacis a foederatis Belgis*, 1654). The italic is not found in England in the sixteenth century, but it is a Fell type. On a poster issued by the Oxford University Press on the occasion of their exhibition at Messrs. Bumpus in November 1930, written by Mr. Morison, the type was shown, and it is there explained that in the Oxford Specimen Book of 1693 it appeared with the wrong upper case.

In his later life Granjon worked at Rome, among others for the New Vatican Press. His work there seems to have been chiefly on oriental types. However, the Corsivo Grosso shown in the *Indice de'caratteri* of that press, issued in 1628, has Granjon characteristics, and has been attributed to that designer by Updike.[1]

[1] On Granjon's italics, see also *The Library*, March 1941, pp. 291–7.

CHAPTER SIX

Italic Type

IN THE EIGHTEENTH CENTURY

AT THE CLOSE of the sixteenth century books set entirely in italic, especially books of verse, were still common. But there was already one indication that the cursives were becoming the servant of roman; they were being cast on the same body as the romans. In Christopher Plantin's specimen of 1567 the two families are shown quite separately, but on the specimen sheet issued by the Egenolff-Berner foundry of Frankfurt in 1592 each example of roman is followed by one of italic on the same body. Nevertheless there was as yet no attempt to harmonise the two designs, and throughout the seventeenth century, italic was still used independently. The first editions of the plays of Racine may be cited as examples, e.g. the *Esther*, 1689, and the *Athalie*, 1691, both printed in italic by Denis Thierry at Paris. These seventeenth-century italics were what we know as old face, cursives of a decided slope and with an inclined but irregular upper case. Irregularity of the angle of inclination in both upper and lower case, was a general characteristic. Most of the letters, in the initial and final strokes, continued the cursive quality of the hands after which they were originally designed. One of the few surviving types of the distinguished designer of the seventeenth century, Christoffel van Dijk, is an italic of this school, a vigorous design cut without any idea of accompanying a roman, however it might be used.[1] In England, from John Day to William Caslon, all designers were content to follow continental models.

The reform, if it may be so called, begins with Philippe Grandjean's "romain du roi", with the first step in the evolution of the modern-face roman. But already in the first half of the seventeenth century there is one peculiar italic which may be recorded, as being in some ways a forerunner of later developments. Updike, in his *Printing Types*, vol. II, p. 19, refers to a curiously condensed cursive found in the preface to an Elzevier book of 1631, P. Cluverius, *Germania Antiqua*, and says that it is "quite a new note in italic type". The fount is shown in the specimen issued by Johannes Elzevier in 1658, and again in the sale catalogue of the types of Abraham Elzevier of 1713, where its size is described as Dubbelde Mediaan. Charles Enschedé, in an essay included in the specimen of *Die hochdeutschen Schriften*, published by Messrs. Enschedé in 1919, mentions the type but had not discovered the founder. According to Enschedé it was cut neither by Van Dijk nor by the Luther foundry at Frankfurt. It is not surprising to find that it was in common use in England from about 1650 to 1720, during a period in which many Dutch types were being imported. It occurs in the sale catalogue of the James Foundry, 1782, as double pica. It is especially common as a heading type on official documents issued by the King's printers. The most striking peculiarity of the type is its condensation, and in order to achieve the condensation the designer has romanised some of his letters; notably the m and the n, in which the shoulders are squared up. The a also is a rounder letter, though condensed, than the typical old-face a.

In the case of this unusual fount the romanising appears to be accidental, due to the effort at condensation. On the other hand, with Grandjean's italic we find a deliberate attempt to make the secondary type conform to the roman. He designed his a, m and n like those letters in the Elzevier fount; one effect of these forms was

[1] For its use in prefatory matter, see C. Salmasius, *Plinianæ Exercitationes*, Utrecht, 1689.

to remove some of the irregularity of slope from the lower case. In the upper case he also gave a more consistent slope to his letters. In the old-face italics the inconsistency of inclination was not in itself unpleasing, except where the capitals were composed together. But when considered in relation to roman the effect might be disturbing. That Grandjean, when designing his cursive, had in mind the roman, is shown by the fact that he introduced the straight-shanked h, a form new in italic. His v too was new, at least in typography, and remained a form peculiar to the eighteenth century. Grandjean's successor at the Imprimerie Royale had by 1712 carried the matter a little further. Grandjean had not altered the cursive beginning strokes of the lower-case letters. Alexandre reduced these strokes until they were something half-way between serifs and the pen-strokes of the old face.

Pierre Simon Fournier makes a few interesting remarks on the subject of italic in the "Avis" to his *Modèles de caractères* of 1742. He calls attention to the great difference between his italic and all preceding designs, and says that he has made his italic more like contemporary writing, meaning the formal hands of the engravers. He then adds that he has distinguished "bien surtout les pleins et deliés", the thick and thin strokes. In his treatment of the serifs he was responsible for an important innovation, namely the introduction of roman serifs on lower-case letters such as m, n, p and r. In the splendid examples of his italics shown in the *Modèles* of 1742 these serifs are inclined and bracketed. He has taken over all the changes introduced by the punch-cutters of the Imprimerie Royale. With the addition of the roman serifs, the absence of tied letters and the regularity of the inclination, Fournier carried the idea of conformity with roman further than any earlier designer (see fig. 34). It should be added that possibly, in the matter of serifs, he had been preceded by Louis Luce, who showed a similar italic in his specimen of 1771 and complained that his designs had been copied as early as 1732. However, Fournier in his *Manuel Typographique* claims originality for his italic. Fournier's excellent design became popular and may be called the characteristic cursive of continental printers of the middle years of the eighteenth century. All French specimen books of that period show these italics with bracketed serifs. The chief designers in other countries (not including England), e.g. Rosart in the Netherlands, and especially Bodoni in Italy, followed the Fournier model.

ITALIQUE.

OTHON lui livre la bataille, &
la perd : il avoit pourtant encore as-
sez de forces pour faire tête à l'en-
nemi ; mais quelque chose que
pûssent lui dire ſes ſoldats, dont il
étoit extrémement cheri, pour l'en-
gager à hazarder une ſeconde ba-
taille, il aima mieux mourir ge-
nereusement que de répandre davan-
tage le ſang de ſes Sujets. Après
avoir dormi toute la nuit d'un pro-
fond ſommeil, il ſe passa ſon épée
au travers du corps, étant dans la
trente-huitiéme année de ſon âge, &
le troisiéme mois de ſon Empire.

Fig. 34. Fournier's Italic.

Popular as the Fournier italics were, they were comparatively short-lived. Soon after Fournier's death, the great founders of the Didot family completed Grandjean's work and cut the first fully developed modern-face romans. As a secondary letter they designed an italic with still less of its original calligraphic quality. In 1784 Pierre Didot l'ainé issued his *Épître sur les progrès de l'imprimerie* printed in an italic designed by his brother Firmin at the age of nineteen (see figs. 35, 36). This fact we learn from the notes to the *Épître*. In 1786 Pierre published a second edition along with his *Essai de nouvelles fables*, and with additional notes. He states

ÉPÎTRE

SUR

LES PROGRÈS

DE L'IMPRIMERIE.

PAR DIDOT, FILS AÎNÉ.

A PARIS,

IMPRIMÉ CHEZ DIDOT L'AÎNÉ,

avec les italiques de FIRMIN*, son second fils.*

M. DCC. LXXXIV.

Fig. 35. Didot's Modern Face

that Firmin, who was born in 1764, had cut the italic of the first edition, a 12 pt., and since then the 8 pt. of the notes of the second edition and the 10 pt. of the "Approbation". The larger italic of 1784—it had appeared already in 1783 in F. A. Didot's editions of Corneille, of Racine, and of Fénelon's *Télémaque*—was especially commended by Mr. Stanley Morison in an article in *The Fleuron*, no. 5, "Towards an Ideal Italic". This article was written from a special point of view, the ideal being a perfect harmony with roman. He finds that the Didot letter approaches nearer to being an inclined roman than any previous cursive. He notices the absence of foot serifs to the p and q as being a relic of a calligraphic fount. The top serifs to the lower-case letters are again roman, but not bracketed like Fournier's. They are flat, both above and below, to harmonise with the serifs of the modern-face roman. In addition to the almost mechanical regularity of the slope, the colour is lighter than in Fournier's design. The lighter typography of the eighteenth century was unfavourable to italic, which could not support further loss of colour. This side of the degradation of italic is illustrated by Fleischman's cursives. That founder has been accused of taking all the life out of his types, an accusation which is certainly well founded in the case of his italics. Firmin Didot himself went on to design modern-face romans of a more abrupt modelling, with a greater contrast between the thick and the thin strokes, and accordingly produced heavier and more abruptly modelled italics. These are to be seen in the well-known Louvre editions printed by his brother Pierre towards the end of the century. The flat serifs, however, remained, were generally copied and will be found in the specimen books of most continental founders of the next generation. Bodoni of course adopted the new fashion, and a little later we find the German founder, Erich Walbaum, whose modern-face roman has recently returned to favour, cutting an italic in the Didot style. The specimens of Gillé fils *c.* 1808 (reproduced in *The Fleuron*, no. 6), of N. P. Gando of *c.* 1810 (reproduced by Messrs. Enschedé in 1917) and of Molé le jeune, 1819 (shown in Updike, fig. 322) all illustrate the way in which Didot had revolutionised the design of italic. In the

ÉPÎTRE
SUR LES PROGRÈS
DE L'IMPRIMERIE.

A MON PERE.

CET art qui tous les jours multiplie avec grace
Et les vers de Virgile et les leçons d'Horace;
Qui, plus sublime encor, plus noble en son emploi,
Donne un texte épuré des livres de la Loi,
Et, parmi nous de Dieu conservant les oracles,
Pour la religion fit ses premiers miracles;
Des grands événements cet art conservateur,
Trop ingrat seulement envers son inventeur,
N'a pas su nous transmettre avec pleine assurance
Le génie étonnant qui lui donna naissance.
Toi qui sus concevoir tant de plans à la fois,
A l'immortalité pourquoi perdre tes droits?

Fig. 36. Didot's Italic, 1783

printers' specimens of Carl Wolf at Munich, 1825, and of Carl Tauchnitz, Leipzig, of the same year, we can trace the popularity of the modern style in Germany.

Meanwhile the Didots had in part reversed their style. They had given up the roman serifs and designed the lifeless italics which were ultimately to prevail in the nineteenth century. Firmin Didot's new italic may be seen in the specimen issued by the Imprimerie in 1812, and that of his brother in his specimen of 1819. Both have given up the roman serifs and have produced cursives of mechanical rigidity, with no life of their own, and not intended to be used on their own. The "Avis" to Pierre Didot's specimen is set in one of these spineless letters, and the reader is immediately conscious that this is only an introduction and that he will not be expected to read a book in such a type. However, the Didots, if their intention was to kill italic as an independent letter, had attained that end. Although italics with flat roman serifs continued to be used for some years—the Imprimerie displayed them in a specimen of 1855—it was the latest of the Didot designs that was destined to survive.

In England during the eighteenth century the design of italic followed a similar course and met the same end. There is one exception to be noted: roman serifs never appeared on an English italic. Such cursives are occasionally found in an English printed book, but were, I believe, imported types; at least they are not to be found in the extant specimen books of English founders.[1] As in the case of the modern-face roman, the beginning of the revolution is to be traced to John Baskerville. His italic has received much less praise than his roman; it has been described as pinched and wiry. But the use made of the Monotype version in our day by the Harvard University Press in their edition of the Boswell papers, suggests that it has been underrated. Baskerville's italic is more evenly sloped than the old face; it has the rounded a, the m and the n shaped as in Grandjean's type; from that source too he has copied the straight-shanked h, though he has not taken over the v;

[1] See Thomas Maurice, *An Elegiac and historical poem*, 1795, and *The Feudal Hall. A poem by Agrestis*. T. Bensley, 1815.

that eighteenth-century letter is absent from English cursives. The g and the s are other letters which bring the Baskerville lower case into closer harmony with the roman. On the other hand, he has inconsistently retained some calligraphic letters in the upper case, e.g. the K and the N. Baskerville's italic influenced the design of cursives in England for the next half-century, until the introduction of the modern face. We can trace that influence in the specimen sheet of Isaac Moore of Bristol, 1768, and in those of Alexander Wilson of Glasgow. The italic of William Martin, the last of the type designers in the transitional period, is even more Baskervillian than his roman. There is in fact only one other design of the period which requires special comment, that of Richard Austin, type-cutter in John Bell's British Letter Foundry established in 1786. Mr. Morison particularly commends the Austin italic on the ground of its harmony with the roman. He finds that the type is of even slope and "carries into it the characteristics of the roman", especially in the matter of serif treatment. The serifs of the capitals are not the unbracketed serifs of the nineteenth century, but are carefully shaped in an arc on the under side. As to the lower case the type is very like Baskerville's, though less pinched, while some of the swash capitals are clearly derived from that source. The individuality of the serif treatment, the re-introduction of the rounded h (the straight-shanked h was also supplied) and other small details separate Austin's italic from the nineteenth-century design.

The final step towards the modern italic was taken about 1800 by Robert Thorne. In his specimen of 1803 the new modern-face romans, one of them dated 1800, are accompanied by italics which are in several ways parallel to the later work of the Didots in France. The serifs of the upper case and of the ascenders of the lower case are flat and unbracketed; cursive beginning strokes are still retained, as in all English italics, but have quite lost the quality of flowing pen-strokes. The mechanical regularity of the slope adds to the lifelessness of Thorne's design. Finally the tendency to over-modelling, characteristic of nineteenth-century types, is already in evidence. The other London founders rapidly followed Thorne's example. As the English founders missed the stage of cursives with roman serifs, they arrived at the modern italic even before their French colleagues.

APPENDIX

LIST OF BOOKS PRINTED AT ROME BY VICENTINO, 1524–7

1 G. G. Trissino, *Canzone*, s.n. (spring of 1524).

2 *Coryciana*, Ed. B. Palladius. Vicentino and Lautizio Perugino, July 1524.

3 G. G. Trissino, *La Sophonisba*. Vicentino and Lautizio, July 1524 (other issues, September 1524).

4 — *Oratione . . . al serenissimo Principe di Venetia*. Vicentino and Lautizio, October 1524.

5 — *I Ritratti*. Vicentino and Lautizio, October 1524.

6 C. Silvanus Germanicus, *In Pontificatum Clementis Septimi pont. max. panegyris*. Vicentino and Lautizio, December 21, 1524 (Vict. & Alb. Mus.).

7 G. G. Trissino, *Epistola de la vita che dee tenere una donna vedova*. Vicentino and Lautizio, 1524.

8 — *Epistola de le lettere nuovamente aggiunte ne la lingua italiana*, s.n.

9 B. Casalius, *In legem agrariam . . . oratio*. Vicentino and Lautizio, 1524.

10 G. Sauromanus, *De religione ac communi concordia*, 1524.

11 P. Aretino, *Laude di Clemente vii*. Vicentino and Lautizio, December 1524.

12 — *Esortatione della pace fra l'Imperatore e il Re di Francia*. Vicentino and Lautizio, 1524.

13 A. Firenzuola, *Discacciamento de le nuoue lettere inutilmente aggiunte*. Vicentino and Lautizio, December 1524.

14 A. Franci, *De le lettere nuovamente aggiunte*. Vicentino and Lautizio, s.n.

15 *Bulla Clementis Papae Septimi contra homocidas*. Vicentino and Lautizio (dated Prid. Idib. Junii 1524).

16 Z. Ferrerius, *Hymni novi ecclesiastici*. Vicentino and Lautizio, Kal. Feb. 1525.

17 P. Cursius, *Poema de civitate Castellana faliscorun*. Vicentino and Lautizio, March 29, 1525.

18 C. Marcellus, *In Psalmum usque quo Domine oblivisceris me*. Vicentino and Lautizio, April 12, 1525.

19 P. Aretino, *Canzone in laude del sig. Datario*. 1525.

20 P. Collenuccio, *Specchio di Esopo*. Vicentino, 1526.

21 — *Apologi IIII*. Vicentino, 1526.

22 *Panegirico di Francesco* (*Cattani*) *de Diaeceto*. Vicentino, 1526.

23 Pope Julius II, *Oratio de pace*. Vicentino, 1526.

24 *Itinerarium Philippi Belluccii*. Vicentino, s.n.

25 H. Vida, *De Arte Poetica*. Vicentino, May 1527.

26 (A letter dated 8 June, 1527, from Pope Clement VII to the general of the invading army).[1]

The three works by Aretino are quoted from Mazzuchelli's *Vita di Pietro Aretino*. There is a copy of no. 6 in the Victoria and Albert Museum and of all the others there are copies in the British Museum. Nos. 1–19 are printed in Vicentino's first italic, nos. 19–26 in his second type.

[1] Assigned to Vicentino by C. A. Scarafoni in *La Bibliofilia*, 1938, p. 46, *seq*. He mentions further another document, *Pepetuatio officiorum etiam Romanae Curiae*, Vicentino, 1525. Both are in the Biblioteca Vittorio Emanuele.

CHAPTER SEVEN

Script Type

A SCRIPT TYPE is one cut in imitation of current handwriting, not of the cursive book hands, but of the ordinary script in everyday use. The Bastardas, Fraktur and italic were, after all, book hands. As there may be varying degrees of currency, it might be expected that there would be types on the border-line between the two groups, which might be placed in either. There are a few such types, but on the whole this difficulty does not arise. In modern usage the script is intended for the printing of tickets, circular letters, cards, paper money, etc., and such was the intention of Fournier as laid down in the specimen of his "bâtarde coulée" of 1749. But almost all the early scripts were cut as book types and were used as such; for example, Hans Kilian's Kanzleischrift, Granjon's civilité, and Pierre Moreau's bâtarde. As the scripts are based on current handwriting, they fall, like the hands, into the two divisions of gothic or mediaeval, and Latin or Renaissance. The Germans still write a gothic hand, and there are traces of gothic in French hands of the eighteenth century, apart from survivals or revivals of civilité. Pure Latin scripts are curiously late in their appearance; there are none recorded before the seventeenth century.

GOTHIC SCRIPTS

In the second part of Vicentino's writing book, published about 1525, among other hands there is shown a "Lettera da bolle", that is the script used for the writing of Bulls, or at least derived from

Quare mediante eodem Commissario supplicari fecerunt humiliter
tem habentes de opportune dispensationis gratia misericorditer pro
mmissa fuit eorum in hac parte supplicationibus inclinati Aucte
e per p̄ntes manu Commissarij nr̄i et Notarij infrātorum subscri
abrice de certo subsidio ad illius utilitatem ac opus ipsum prosequen
datum subministraverunt qd impedimento Tertij et Quarti graduum
non obstante libere valeant inter se mr̄imonium contrahere et in eo postq̄
modo dicta mulier propter hoc ab aliquo rapta non fuerit prolem
p̄ntes omnibus et singulis ad quos spectat ne sub excōis et Quin
onentes sic dispensatos postq̄ ut prefertur dispensati fuerint quovis
ant sine presumant Datum

Fig. 37. Lettera da Bolle

that script. This is an upright, round, gothic hand, which in the lower case has some resemblance to Schwabacher, or to the later French hand called Ronde. The form was established by tradition and most of the Italian calligraphers, who published their work, display a specimen. That the hand was cut as a type has apparently not been recorded hitherto (see fig. 37). There is in the British Museum a single sheet of vellum set in a type which is a faithful transcript of the "lettera da bolle". The type area measures about 200 mm. by 300 mm. The text is a form, with blanks not filled in, granting a licence to marriage within the prohibited degrees. It was issued by the "Collegium della Fabrica di S. Pietro". This College of sixty members was set up by a Bull of Pope Clement VII dated December 12, 1523, for the purpose of the completion of the building of St. Peter's in Rome. Their privilege to grant the kind of licence of which our sheet is the subject was given to the College by Pope Paul III in a Bull dated February 3, 1542. The printed document cannot then be earlier than 1542, but it has the appearance of being not much later. The word Collegium at the head is set in a line of curious, rather ugly, initials, which again can be paralleled in contemporary writing books. The initial C includes a woodcut of St. Peter, which certainly looks like work of the sixteenth century. The sheet then was probably printed about 1550, and the printer would no doubt be the official church typographer, Antonio Blado. It seems likely that a search in Roman archives would bring to light other specimens of the use of this remarkable type.

In 1525 Eustachio Celebrino, a wood-cutter and calligrapher among other things, published at Venice a little book showing the "Lettera mercantesca", a gothic script; it may be recalled that even in Italy, as late as the middle of the sixteenth century, a variety of gothic hands still survived, as may be seen in the popular writing manual of Palatino at Rome. Conservative commercial circles were still using mediaeval hands. As has been pointed out in the case of roman and italic, it was the humanistic scholars who were responsible for the Renaissance hands, whether in the manuscript or the printed book.

This particular variety, the "Lettera mercantesca", was translated into type, although very little used. It stood no chance as a book hand against the many fine cursives of the Vicentino school now at the disposal of Italian printers, and the day for paper money and the other modern uses of the script had not yet arrived. The "mercantesca" type seems to be due to another writing-master, Domenico Manzoni, who published at Venice in 1546 a school primer entitled *Libretto molto utile per imparar a leggere, scriuere & abaco*. About half a page of this small book, printed by Comin da Trino, is set in the script. A few other books by Manzoni contain some words in the type, e.g. his *Abachetto nuovo*, 1553 (see D. E. Smith's *Rara Arithmetica*, p. 257), and *La brieve risolutione di aritmetica*, 1553. Probably also his later manual of 1564 recorded in Destailleur's *Catalogue de livres rares*, 1891, contains some of the type.

After these early experiments the Italians appear to have cut no gothic scripts, nor Latin either before the time of Bodoni. North of the Alps we have to trace the German Currentschrift, the French civilité with its Netherlands branch, and the English secretary.

In sixteenth-century Germany the calligraphic books of the writing-masters show that beside the ordinary Currentschrift there were various Kanzleischriften, more formal scripts used in the German Chanceries. Some are very like Fraktur, while others are even more fanciful, described as "gebrochene", the original meaning of Fraktur. Caspar Neff's book, Cologne, 1549, with a later edition, 1580, shows specimens of Kanzlei which are "zuruchgebogene", inclined to the left, "hangende", inclined to the right, and "gewundene" which may be translated as tortured. Two of these varieties were cut as types, the two earliest gothic scripts in Germany. A printer at Hamburg, Joachim Louwe (1548–69), had a "gebrochene hangende Kanzleischrift", of which a reproduction is given in J. M. Lappenberg's *Zur Geschichte der Buchdruckerkunst in Hamburg*, 1840, p. 30. There are three sizes. The *Liber de purgatorio* of Johannes Aepinus, with the imprint Londinii, 1549, has a sheet of Errata at the end in this "Kanzleischrift", and must have been printed at Hamburg, although the main part of the book was printed by Richard Grafton. The author's preface is dated from Hamburg. The other Kanzleischrift, the earlier in date, is a more handsome letter, one of the best scripts ever designed.

Crous and Kirchner, *op. cit.*, give a reproduction (Abb. 98) from the *Friedschirmsbuch* of Marsilius of Padua, printed by Hans Kilian at Neuburg on the Danube in 1545. The letter is found used occasionally in several books of Kilian's, and in 1557 the whole text of his edition of the German version of Donato Gianotti's history of Venice is set in the script. The type is "zuruchgebogene"; some of the down-strokes are bent backwards, although the type as a whole may be described as upright. The capitals are Fraktur. Close parallels to both these Kanzleischriften may be seen in Neff's writing book. Kilian's type was used later at Laugingen by E. Salzer (see A. Schiess, *Kurtze verzaichnus der fürnembsten Historien*, 1564).

The next script, a more usual Schreibschrift, is that of Christopher Froschouer the Younger of Zürich, used in the German edition of Hans Bluom's architectural work, *Ein kunstrich Buch von allerley Antiquiteten*, 1567. Bluom's work on the five orders of classical columns appeared first in Latin in 1550, printed by Froschouer, and was succeeded by many other editions, illustrated with woodcuts by the author. Updike gives a reproduction from the German edition (his fig. 77) from which it appears that the script was used for part of the text along with a Schwabacher. It has sufficient colour to go with that black letter. Although it represents a contemporary German hand, the printer was no doubt influenced by Granjon's civilité, which had by this time won considerable popularity. An early Berlin newspaper, 1626, in Schreibschrift is shown in K. F. Bauer's *Aventur und Kunst*, 1940, p. 166. After these sixteenth-century examples I find no other until the Frankfurt script of about a hundred years later. This appears first on the specimen of Reinhard Voskens, undated, but about 1660. It is found also on other Frankfurt sheets, that of Stubenvoll, 1713, and J. F. Halle, 1727. The Enschedés have the type and it is shown in their *Hochdeutsche Schriften*, 1919. They consider that it came from the Luther foundry, and no doubt that foundry also had matrices, but Voskens seems to have cut the original punches. Probably this Voskens is identical with the brother of Bartholomeus Voskens. The two brothers started their famous foundry at Amsterdam in 1641, and by 1646 it is known that they had parted.

This Frankfurt Currentschrift was not known to Faulmann, who in his *Illustrierte Geschichte der Buchdruckerkunst* describes the earliest German scripts as those of Christian Zingk of Wittenberg, cut early in the eighteenth century after the hand of Schmotther, and of Christian Porsdorff at Leipzig, 1722. He says that an edition of Luther's *Katechismus* was printed at Eisenberg by J. Z. Fleischer in 1725 in this script. Perhaps the German printers used their scripts more in the modern fashion for ephemeral publications, since remarkably few books have been recorded set in script types. The "Cursive allemand" shown by Fournier was procured from the Leipzig founder, Breitkopf, but it appears to date from the previous century, as Fournier says that books were printed from the script at Nuremberg about 1695. The Schreibschriften of the eighteenth century, such as the two examples shown in the Enschedé specimen, one dated 1772 and the second cut by Unger, illustrate the evolution of the German current handwriting. Unger's script has become much lighter and simpler than Froschouer's, though little changed in design. Breitkopf also had a lighter design shown in his specimen of 1786 of which a reproduction is given in *Ars Typographica*, vol. II, no. 2. The latest script shown by the Enschedés, the "Klein Kanon", of unknown origin, has lost all colour; it corresponds among gothic scripts to Didot's "Anglaise" among the Latin. It is like the Anglaise not only in colour, but also in the attempt to conceal the fact that it is type by the close fitting of the connecting strokes. Again, like Anglaise among the Latin scripts, it remained the standard script throughout the nineteenth century.

The Viennese founder, J. T. Trattner, in his specimen of 1787, displays three scripts, one the usual Currentschrift, the second a Latin script, and the third a Kanzleischrift. A letter similar to this last appears in a specimen of 1796, showing the work of another Viennese founder, J. L. Kurzbock (died 1792);[1] this is an upright script, a late survival of the gothic chancery hands, and may be compared with the French Ronde. In contrast with the earlier Kanzleischriften, Trattner's specimen has been modified in the direction of the Latin hands.

In 1557 Robert Granjon settled in Lyons and began to print there in a gothic script of his own design. The first book in this type was a French version from Innocenzo Ringhieri, entitled *Dialogue de la vie et de la mort*, and in the dedication Granjon explains his intention in cutting this new design which he calls "lettres françaises" (see fig. 32). Since other countries had national designs for books in their own language, so he considered that the French should have a type based on the national hand for books in French. However, the hand which he translated into type was not the old French book hand, the "lettre bâtarde", but the contemporary current script. This is an indication that the "lettre bâtarde" was a script of the past, which had now passed out of use. Books had ceased to be hand-written and Granjon, in his attempt to introduce a rival to italic, was too late; the book types were already decided, and what he designed proved only an historical curiosity in typography, which is after all what most of the script types are. They have no bearing on the development of our principal book faces.

The popular and lasting name for the type was derived from the titles of two books among the earliest to be printed in the new letter, an edition of Erasmus's *La Civilité puerile*, Jean Bellère, Antwerp, 1559, and *La Civile honesteté pour les enfans*, R. Breton, Paris, 1560. Civilité in this connection means "good manners", and a number of educational books treating of manners and of the art of writing came to be printed in civilité. It was thought to be an advantage that children should learn to read from a book printed in a type resembling the ordinary current script.

Between 1557 and 1562 Granjon printed some twenty books in his new type. In *P. Galtheri Alexandreidos libri decem*, there is printed a privilege, dated December 26, 1557, granted by Henri II,

[1] Shown in A. Mayer's *Wiens Buchdrucker Geschichte*.

giving Granjon a monopoly of his design for ten years. The privilege, as often, seems to have made little difference, for in 1559 two Paris printers, Richard Breton and Philippe Danfrie, began printing in a close copy of Granjon's civilité. A list of books in their civilité is given by E. Picot in his *Note sur G. Richardière et Ph. Danfrie*. Picot says that Granjon allowed this Paris firm to make use of his privileged letter, but gives no authority for the assertion; at any rate their design is a copy and not the original Granjon. Another Paris variety appears in the writing book of Pierre Hamon, 1561, where some introductory verses are set in civilité. In the meantime Granjon had supplied his type to Guillaume Silvius and to Plantin at Antwerp. Plantin had three civilités cut by Granjon, two of which appear in his *Index Characterum* of 1567, one being identical with that used in Granjon's own books, and the other, a larger and more formal design. Granjon was living in Antwerp in 1565 and 1566, and in 1565 an edition of L. Vivé's *Introduction de philosophie divine* was printed by Silvius with Granjon's name and device on the title-page.[1]

Granjon's script did not win great popularity in France, although used occasionally at all periods. Philippe Danfrie's *Graphomètre*, Paris, 1597, shows a larger design, rather more like the later hand known as Ronde. Another Paris printer, Claude Micard, printed P. Habert's *Le Chemin de bien vivre*, 1597, in another civilité. Habert's is again a book of manners and writing. At Lyons Jean de Tournes used a few words of the original Granjon script in his *Calendrier Historial*, 1563; Jean de Tournes II had two civilités, neither of them the original Granjon; the smaller was used in *La Galatée*, Geneva, 1598, and the larger in C. Guichard, *Funerailles des Rommains*, 1581. The type of the Guichard survived at Lyons and appears in the Delacolonge specimen of 1773. Civilité never entirely dropped out of use in France, and examples are shown in many specimen books of the eighteenth century; there is an excellent specimen in Claude Lamesle's book

[1] See a reproduction in Sabbe and Audin, *Die Civilité Schriften des R. Granjon*, Vienna, 1929. This book shows a dozen different civilités, from Granjon to Perrin, French and Flemish.

of 1742, and Fournier, of course, shows one. Finally, Louis Perrin at Lyons in the middle of the nineteenth century printed J. Soulary's *Sonnets humouristiques* in civilité. By Fournier's day the script no longer represented the current hand of the French, which had become Latin, and MM. Sabbe and Audin point out that the compositors often confuse certain letters.

Civilité enjoyed a greater popularity in the Netherlands, more particularly in a variety based on the contemporary Flemish hand. Aimé Tavernier of Bailleul, who was a founder and printer at Antwerp, had produced his Flemish design by 1559, an imitation of Granjon. Plantin, too, besides the scripts cut by Granjon, had others from Flemish founders.[1] The Enschedés possess six founts of civilité dating from the sixteenth century, which they display in their specimen of 1926. Two were cut by Tavernier, and two others, with perhaps a third, by Henric van der Keere, founder at Ghent. The sixth may, perhaps, be a Granjon. It was used by Plantin and was possibly the third of the civilités which he bought from the original designer. The two sizes of "geschreven" shown on the specimen sheet of the widow of Dirk Voskens, *c.* 1700, appear to be Tavernier's; they are the same as those shown on pls. 17 and 18 of Sabbe and Audin.

Of French civilités in general it may be said that the type was never a practical one. Granjon's intention of introducing a new "lettre française" entirely failed. In order to carry out the idea of imitating a script many extra ligatures had to be cut; there were often three or more varieties for one letter; there was an initial m, a medial m and a final m. The long s and the f were very thick in the face and too conspicuous on the page. The French design is better than the Flemish, which has a restless appearance like the German Currentschrift, because of its lack of a prevailing direction of the strokes.

GOTHIC SCRIPTS IN ENGLAND

From Martin Billingsley, who published his calligraphic work *The Pen's Excellence* in 1618, we learn that at that time the normal

[1] For details, see Sabbe and Audin, *op. cit.*, and also for references to books printed in the Netherlands in civilité.

handwriting of commercial circles was a gothic script, the secretary hand. As this script was not superseded by the Italian hand until well into the seventeenth century, it is rather surprising that there are not more traces of its influence in typography. The secretary hand had, in fact, its counterpart among our types, but for some reason or other the type was not used for the printing of books, as was the contemporary civilité in France and the Netherlands, but on ephemeral circulars and notices in the manner in which script types are used today. Specimens are consequently hard to find, and the subject has not been treated at all fully. Some account of such types is to be found in Sir Hilary Jenkinson's article on "English Current Writing" in the *Transactions of the Bibliographical Society*, vol. XIII, 1915, and there the type is not, of course, the main subject of the research. There were at least three of these secretary types, but only one has, I believe, so far been reproduced.

It may be noted that the term secretary has been used in typography to denote various gothic Bastard types of the same family as Caxton's. It seems better to confine the term to the script based on the Elizabethan current hand, such as was shown by John Baildon in the earliest English writing book of 1571, and which Baildon calls the secretary hand. It was a hand used throughout Europe, with national peculiarities, in Italy as well as in the countries north of the Alps. In Italy it was called "lettera francese" or "lettera mercantesca", as we have seen from the little book of the Venetian calligrapher, Eustachio Celebrino. In France and the Netherlands it was known as civilité. There was actually one book printed in Edinburgh in one of Granjon's civilités, an edition of Æsop printed by Thomas Bassandyne in 1571, and a single sheet, a Privy Council instruction, 1575, relating to the compulsory purchase of a Bible.

A genuine English script was apparently not cut until towards the end of the century. From 1576 we find one in use first by Bynneman and then by the King's printer, Christopher Barker, who was, in 1599, succeeded by his son Robert, the printer of the Authorised Version of the Bible. The type appears first in the colophon of A. Guarna's *Bellum grammaticale*, Bynneman, 1576; it was next used for the printing of various official and semi-official notices, in which certain portions were to be filled in by hand. Sir Hilary Jenkinson, in the article referred to above, reproduced part of a wine licence issued by Sir Walter Raleigh under the monopoly granted to him on May 4, twenty-fifth year of Elizabeth, i.e. 1583, and renewed on August 9, 1588. In the Record Office there are hundreds of these licences printed in secretary, in a number of different settings. The printed forms were available soon after the date of the granting of the monopoly, the earliest noted being filled in for June 20, 1583. In the Record Office, also in the same secretary, are many bundles of recognisances entered into by victuallers, of which the earliest noted date from the forty-second year of Elizabeth, i.e. 1599–1600. Sir Hilary Jenkinson refers also to marriage licences as being set in the same type. In one series of documents it was used on the King's business, on circular letters demanding loans, the earliest preserved being issued in the second year of James I, July 31, 1604. Editions for the ninth and eleventh year are also preserved. One of the most interesting documents printed in the script is one relating to the affairs of John Stowe, the chronicler and antiquary. This is an epitome of the letters patent issued on March 6, 1604, authorising Stowe to "collect voluntary contributions and kind gratitudes" in relief of his continued poverty.[1]

This secretary came into the possession of the Grover foundry, and thence to the James foundry. In the Sale Catalogue and Specimen of that foundry of 1782, it is shown under the title "Great Primer Secretary", along with Union Pearl, the Ichabod Dawks cursorials, and other scripts. Most of the curious matrices were acquired by Dr. Edmund Fry, descended to the Fann Street foundry, and so came into the hands of T. B. Reed, the author of *The Old English Letter Foundries*. But by that time the Great

[1] Other sheets printed in this secretary No. 1 are a proclamation of the thirty-fifth year of Elizabeth's reign, headed "Abuses used concerning the heawing, sawing and measuring of timber" (Lansdowne MSS., vol. 161, no. 22), and "A Brief of the Bill concerning Printers" (Ames Collection of Title-pages, vol. 1, p. 58), which relates to an Act of 1614 restricting the importation of books.

Primer Secretary had disappeared. A Dutch origin has been suggested for the type. It so happens that through the publications of Messrs. Enschedé, of Haarlem, the Plantin Museum at Antwerp, and the researches of MM. Sabbe and Audin, we have records and reproductions of a large number of Netherlands civilités. The English secretary differs from all these, and also from the French civilités known to have been in use at Paris and Lyons in the sixteenth century.

The circular letters issued by James I have been mentioned. The issue for the third year of his reign is printed in a different secretary, larger in face, and more upright than the Great Primer. The recognisances of victuallers preserved in the Record Office for the sixteenth year of James I are also in this secretary No. 2. From the seventeenth year of James I onwards, these particular forms are set in roman and italic. The type, however, was still in use, and as late as August 19, 1670, we find a Privy Council notice relating to the infringement of the copyright for law books held by Richard Atkyns, set in type No. 2. This secretary was taken to York, possibly by the King's printer, Robert Barker II, who was summoned by the King to York in 1642. However, the two York documents I have seen are of rather later date, one being a jury list dating from the Commonwealth, in the possession of Messrs. Hodgson, and the other an ecclesiastical document, a licence for probate issued in the diocese of York. The printed form is for 1670, but it is filled in for March 11, 1678.

Some use of secretary No. 2 is found in printed books. The specimens of the secretary hand displayed by the writing-masters of the seventeenth century were usually engraved on copper-plates. But occasionally more elementary school books, consisting mainly of letterpress giving instructions for writing, contain a specimen of secretary printed from type. Edmund Coote's *The English Schoolmaster*, a book which appeared first in 1596, and was reprinted many times throughout the seventeenth century, gives us an example. The early editions include no specimens, or none printed from type. But the editions of 1636, 1662 and 1673 have at the end a specimen of our type No. 2, consisting of an alphabet and a specimen from the Psalms. The edition of 1684, in the place of secretary, shows an Italian hand, printed from an engraved plate. This secretary No. 2 is not known from any type specimen, either English or foreign.

There is still a third fount of secretary, of a still larger size and of more handsome design. This was used for the words in a music book of 1641. Scripts have frequently been used with music; one example was shown by Mr. Morison (*The Fleuron*, no. 4, p. 5) from the press of Sebastien Cramoisy, 1625. The Netherlands type designer, J. F. Rosart, says of a Financière cut by him in 1753, that it was designed "pour servir à la musique". The English work referred to is John Barnard's *Book of Selected Church Musick*, printed by Edward Griffin in 1641. The type appears in no other book from the same press of those preserved in the British Museum, nor have I found it anywhere else. Barnard's book is a handsome production decorated with some fine calligraphic initials and tailpieces. The author's preface is worth quoting for the interesting light it throws on correcting for the press in his day. "If therefore anyone surveying this volume shall find it short of what he expected, or I perhaps purposed, and gave out; To him, let me answer first, that what paines (and I may add watchings) I have sustain'd in gathering, collationing, correcting, revising this that is already done with such wearisome trudging up and downe to the Presse, so farre from my house, if no man can imagine of himselfe, I am sure mine owne overtoyled body, and wasted spirits feele." It is known from other sources also that proof sheets were not usually sent out, but had to be corrected in the printing house.

Besides these secretary types there was another kind of gothic script which survived even longer, a legal script known as court hand. This was a hand of considerable antiquity, of which the history is traced in Sir Hilary Jenkinson's *The Later Court Hands of England*. Its design remained uniform for several centuries, and in the writing books of the calligraphers of the seventeenth century there are a number of fine specimens of the script,[1] an upright

[1] Cf. pl. lxvii in Sir Ambrose Heal's *English Writing Masters*.

hand which appears to be confined to England. Since stereotyped legal phrases are of frequent occurrence in legal documents, the cutting of type with which to print such passages was an obvious convenience, and the type was cut, but does not seem to have been much used. At least, such legal forms of the seventeenth and early eighteenth century in court hand as I have been able to see are either written or printed from plates; for example, writs and subpoenas. The type is only known to me from the James Sale Catalogue, where two sizes are displayed, double pica and English. These are known to have been in the earlier Grover foundry, and

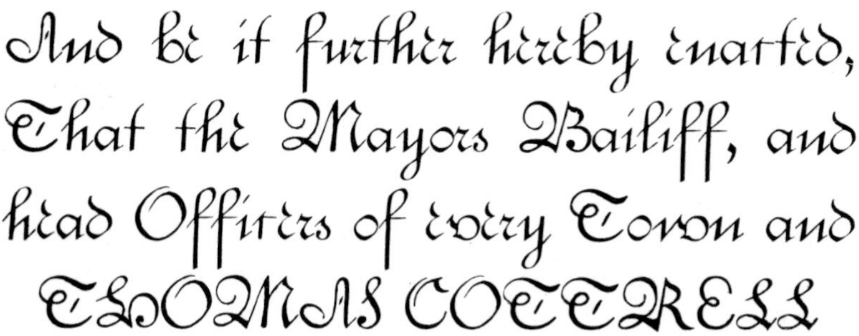

And be it further hereby enacted,
That the Mayors Bailiff, and
head Officers of every Town and
THOMAS COTTRELL

Fig. 38. Cottrell's Engrossing

the matrices of the English size were still in existence in Reed's day, and perhaps still survive. The use of the court hand for legal documents was abolished in 1733 (according to Rowe Mores), and its place taken by the script known as engrossing. In typography, our last English gothic script was a fine specimen of engrossing cut by Thomas Cottrell about 1765 for a law printer, William Richardson, who issued an undated broadside specimen of the "New Printing Type in Imitation of the Law Hand". Cottrell showed it in his specimen book issued about 1766. The type was, like the contemporary French ronde and German Kanzleischrift, somewhat romanised; for example, many of the capitals and the lower case h and r have the roman forms. The secretary types and the court hand are difficult to read for those not versed in sixteenth- and seventeenth-century documents. But Cottrell's script is more legible for us, although a legal hand.

LATIN SCRIPTS

The Latin scripts, that is, those based on the Italian hand, are curiously late in typographical history, and in fact are comparatively rare before the eighteenth century. In the seventeenth century we can record only the types of Pierre Moreau and one English specimen. In his article on script types in no. 4 of *The Fleuron*, Mr. Morison derives the Latin scripts from that variety of the Italian hand known as the Cancellaresca Bastarda. This is a rather less formal and more rounded script than that practised by Vicentino. The Venetian writing-master, Amphiareo Vespasiano, claimed to have been its inventor.

Pierre Moreau was a professional calligrapher in Paris who took to producing engraved books and finally books printed from script types. As in the case of civilités and other early gothic scripts, Moreau's types also were intended for bookwork. Between 1643 and 1648 he printed at least eleven books in these types, of which the earliest was an edition of *L'Imitation de Jesus Christ*, and perhaps the best known, an edition of Virgil's *Æneid* in French (cf. fig. 39). These books were set in three sizes of his "bâtarde italienne". The extract from the Royal Privilege granted to Moreau for the printing of the Virgil, reproduced in Mr. Morison's article, reveals the fact that Moreau had another script of a different style, an upright script descended from civilité, based on the hand known as Ronde. P. S. Fournier's account of Moreau's scripts in the *Manuel Typographique* is somewhat confusing; he describes them as ronde, bâtarde brisée, and bâtarde; the bâtarde brisée seems to be missing, unless it is one size of the bâtarde.

Moreau's types came into the possession of the Paris printer, Denis Thierry, and a fine example of their use by that printer is preserved in the Bagford collection in the British Museum, a prospectus of an edition of L. Moreri's *Grand Dictionaire historique*. Later the types passed to the Collombats, father and son (Mr. Morison records two books), then to J. T. Hérissant, whose widow

Iesus mourant.

Poëme dedié

à la Reyne

Regente.

Quatriesme edition,

Reueuë par l'Autheur en 1647.

A Paris;

De l'Imprimerie inuentée par P. Moreau Me Escriuain Juré à Paris, &
Imprimeur ordinaire du Roy,
deuant l'Horloge du Palais.

1647.

Auec Priuilege de Sa Majesté.

Fig. 39. Moreau's Script

finally sold them in 1787 to the Imprimerie Royale. Apart from their appearance in specimen books issued by the Imprimerie, the types made their last appearance on the paper money, the Assignats, of 1792, a use more in accordance with modern practice as to scripts.

Moreau's books, or some of them, are fairly well known, but the English example of a seventeenth-century Latin script is much more of a rarity. Mr. Morison reproduced a page from *Articles and Rules for the Conduct of His Majesty's Army*, published by Moses Pitt in 1673 and preserved in the Record Office. Another smaller sheet reproduced by Mr. Morison dates from 1672. A third use of the type is found in *Instructions for the better ordering of His Majesty's Fleet*, issued by James, Duke of York as Lord High Admiral, *c.* 1680, 14 folio pages without imprint. The type appears to have been in the hands of the King's printer, but whence it came and where it went is unrecorded. It is a remarkably fine example of an Italian script, and it would be surprising to learn that any contemporary English type-cutter could rise to such heights.

We come now to the "Cursorials" of the Grover (afterwards James) foundry, dating from about 1700. An account of them is given by Rowe Mores in his *Dissertation*, by Reed, and in Mr. Morison's *Ichabod Dawks*. Mores says the "cursorial is a flimsy type imitating a pseudo Italian handwriting, and fitted for ladies and beaux". They are in fact based on an inferior Italian hand, showing some gothic survivals. The Grover foundry possessed six sizes, double pica, great primer, English No. 1, English No. 2, pica and long primer. Of these several are still extant in the foundry of Messrs. Stephenson, Blake & Co., of Sheffield. They descended to the present owners from Rowe Mores through the Fry foundry and the Fann Street foundry (the Reeds). Ichabod Dawks began to print his newsletter in the English No. 2 in 1696. Dawks used also the double pica, and it seems probable that these first cursorials were cut at the instigation of Dawks and for the purpose of reproducing more or less in facsimile the manuscript newsletter which was handed about in the coffee-houses. Two examples of the use of these scripts may be added to those mentioned by Mr. Morison.

The printer, H. Meere, whose specimen sheet (*c.* 1700) shows the smallest size of the cursorials, inserts in *The Observator* of February 7, 1708, a notice of "Scriptographia", which he described as suitable for blank forms. The notice is printed in the pica of the Grover series. The second example is a single sheet poem entitled *Fair Warning*, printed in 1710 by John Baker, set in the double pica size. The word "Scriptographia" in Meere's notice is set in the

A B C D E F F G G H I J K L M N
O P Q R S T T U V W X Y Z
a b b c d d e f g h h i j k l l m n
o p q r s ſ t u v w x y z
& ſh ſt Qu

Fig. 40. Union Pearl, *c.* 1700

Union Pearl of the Grover foundry, and this shaded script is possibly the seventh cursorial referred to by Mores. This type also has survived, but except for the one word in *The Observator* I have found no example of its contemporary use. The whole series, in design inferior to Moreau or the English script of 1672, is of considerable interest as a typographical curiosity.[1]

When we reach the generation of Fournier and Luce, Fleischman and Rosart, the Latin scripts of the continental countries appear in great numbers, far too many to be followed in any detail here. Reproductions will be found in Updike, in Mr. Morison's article, and also in an article by McMurtrie in *Ars Typographica*, vol. II, no. 2. The names of these various scripts become somewhat confusing. There are three groups among the Latin scripts, the

[1] Two sizes of the Grover cursorials and the Union Pearl are shown on the Specimen Sheet of Benjamin Franklin Bache, Philadelphia, which was reproduced in facsimile by McMurtrie in 1925.

ronde, a descendant of civilité which is largely gothic, the bâtarde coulée, also called financière because used in the Ministry of Finance, and the bâtarde ordinaire or italienne, the purest form of Latin script. Fournier uses the word bâtarde alone instead of bâtarde italienne. The financière, originally a more cursive variety of the bâtarde, in the course of time became indistinguishable from it. The three hands, now to all intents and purposes only two, are still shown in the 1819 specimen of the Imprimerie Royale, and the ronde is frequently found as a decorative type in French books of the first half of the nineteenth century. Even German type-cutters were influenced by this flood of scripts and Latin scripts began to appear in Teutonic specimens, for instance in that of J. H. Prentzler of Frankfurt, 1774 (reproduced in McMurtrie). That prolific type designer, G. B. Bodoni, of Parma, naturally copied the French and produced a score of scripts, of no great merit and with bewildering titles. The types which he calls Cancellaresca appear to be little removed from italics, and when he describes them as something new in typography his meaning is obscure. To his ronde he gives the title Inglese, which supports Mr. Morison's assertion that Bodoni knew little about the history of handwriting.

In England, after the cutting of the Grover cursorials, there is a long gap in the history of scripts. Neither William Caslon I, nor his son, nor Baskerville designed anything in this class. Thomas Cottrell, a pupil of Caslon's, whose own foundry was established in 1757, began a new vogue with a script which dated from 1774 (see the reproduction in McMurtrie).[1] He was influenced partly by the French, but introduced an innovation which was in turn copied by the continental founders. Cottrell attempted to produce the illusion of actual script by fitting his letters with exactness. This excess of ingenuity was particularly associated with the English founders, and the type was called Anglaise by its imitators in France, the Didots and others. In England all the other founders soon had their new scripts in the style of Cottrell; it is possible that

[1] See also a reproduction in Berry and Johnson's *English Type Specimen Books*, pl. 21.

one of them even preceded him with the script which was cut for Dr. John Trusler. According to Timperley, Dr. Trusler began his project for printing his sermons in imitation of manuscript as early as 1771.[1] All these types, Cottrell's, Trusler's and that of Caslon, which appeared in 1785, still had considerable traces of the true Italian hand. But after a few years these scripts

The TALE of the BARD.

Turloch lived at Lubar of streams. In deeds of fame his hair grew white. Strangers knew the way to his hall: In the broad path there grew no mountain graſs. No door had he to his gate. 'Why' he said should the wanderer see it shut?—Turloch was tall as the oak of his vale. On either side, a fair branch lifted its green growing head. Two green trees smiling in the shower, and looking thro' rainbows on

Fig. 41. Script, *c.* 1785. Unidentified

became "modern" by a greater differentiation of the thick and thin strokes and increased ingenuity in imitating a current round hand. Then we get the typical Anglaise, admired and copied by the Didots, the script of the nineteenth century. The types of the Cottrell and Trusler class were the last good scripts until we reach the work of the present generation; they perished at the same time as italic, with the introduction of the modern face.

[1] See Mr. Morison's account of Trusler and his type in *The Fleuron*, no. 7.

CHAPTER EIGHT

Early Advertising Types

FAT FACES AND EGYPTIANS[1]

ADVERTISING TYPES, AS distinct from book types, are little more than a century old. The decorated and outline letters of the eighteenth century, popularised by the Paris founder, P. S. Fournier, were intended in the first place for display on title-pages, but in the early years of the nineteenth century English founders designed several types which, however they might be used, were intended for poster work. The earliest of these were the fat faces and Egyptians, both probably due to Robert Thorne, the man who led the way in introducing the modern face into this country.

There are three sources in which one can trace the history of these early display letters; there is first of all the evidence of contemporary writers on typography, secondly, the specimen books of the founders, and thirdly, documents in which the types were actually used. The contemporary writers were naturally at that period not greatly interested in advertising or its typography. They have little to say on the subject, and that little generally contemptuous. Hansard, in his *Typographia*, 1825, shows them as "typographical monstrosities", and in another passage writes of the "folly of fat-faced preposterous disproportions".

He does, however, give us some definite information where he says that "the extremely bold and fat letter, now prevalent in job

[1] See also Nicolette Gray, *XIXth Century Ornamented Types*, 1938.

printing, owes its introduction principally to Mr. Thorne". Savage also, in his *Practical Hints on Decorative Printing*, 1822, says that the fat faces which had entirely changed the appearance of posters were first designed by Robert Thorne. Our second source, the founders' specimens, fails us in the matter of the fat faces, as Thorne himself issued no book of specimens after 1803, and the first display of his jobbing types is in the specimen of his successor,

INDUSTRIAL CITIES OF ENGLAND
and convincing manner, has a direct and

AABCDEFGHIJKLMMNNOPQRS
TUVVWWXYYZ

abcdefghijklmnopqrstuvwxyzfiffflffiffl
1234567890

Quousque

Fig. 42. Thorowgood's Fat Face

William Thorowgood, published in 1820. Vincent Figgins's specimen of 1815 and Fry's of 1816 both show the design, but from our third source we know that it had already been in use for several years before 1815. In the early years of the nineteenth century, the State lotteries were highly popular, and the bills issued by the various contractors who organised the sale of tickets are interesting documents for the history of jobbing types. From the year 1806 onwards, especially on the bills of one of the chief contractors, T. Bish, fat faces are generally used. Again the posters of Drury Lane Theatre adopted the new letter from the year 1807. Whatever the intentions of the original founder, the smaller sizes of the fat faces soon came into use for display in books; examples may be found on the title-page of the *Scot's Magazine* for 1809, and in the *Annual Register* for 1808, issued in 1810. The publishers of the more sensational books, such as reports of murder trials or political trials, as might be expected, found these exaggerated letters suited to their purpose. The political satires and controversial tracts of the bookseller, William Hone, offer many examples of their use.

The fat face was simply Thorne's modern face with the thick strokes swollen out, the thin strokes remaining hair-lines. The thin, flat serifs, the monotonously uniform width of capitals, the vertical stress, and other characteristics of the modern face are repeated. Under this process of fattening, some of the letters became remarkably overweighted; for instance, both the capital and the lower-case G (see fig. 42). In spite of this and notwithstanding the strictures of connoisseurs like Hansard, the type had its uses in display, even in books. The Lee Priory Press, founded in 1813, with the support of Sir Samuel Egerton Brydges, with John Johnson as typographer, was in the forefront of fashion. Its types were all modern, and the use of small sizes of fat faces in headings convinces one that the design was not so preposterous as Hansard asserted. It was taken up by continental founders, and the Imprimerie Royale in Paris even took the—for them—unprecedented step of commissioning Thorne, a foreigner, in 1818, to cut some fat faces for their use as a new form of display type.

The reason for the adoption of the name Egyptian for a particular style of letter is hard to discover. It may be that the heavy squareness of the design in some way reminded the inventor of the style of Egyptian architecture. At any rate, it is clear that he chose a name which was at the time of frequent occurrence in the public press. We may compare the origin of the names Locarno and Zeppelin as applied to two types designed by Professor Koch. There was a considerable revival of the study of Egyptian antiquities in the early years of the nineteenth century, arising out of Napoleon's expedition to Egypt. Archaeologists accompanied the First Consul to the East, and, as a result of their work, the early history of Egypt began to be better known in Western Europe. The Rosetta Stone, which provided the clue to the reading of Egyptian hieroglyphics, was brought to London in 1802, and for some years afterwards, not only the learned periodicals, but also the more popular journals, such as the *Gentleman's Magazine*, included much comment on Egyptian archaeology.

No contemporary writer explicitly states that the type known as Egyptian was originally designed by Robert Thorne, but the name first occurs in connection with his foundry. From the catalogue of the sale of the Thorne foundry, which took place in June 1820, it

ENGLISH ANTIQUE.

Quousque tandem abutere, Catilina, patientia nostra? quamdiu nos etiam furor iste tuus eludet? quem ad finem sese effrenata jactabit audacia? nihilne te nocturnum præsidium palatii, nihil urbis vigiliæ, nihil timor populi, nihil consensus bonorum omnium, nihil hic munitis-
ABCDEFGHIJKLMNOPQRSTU
£1234567890.

Fig. 43. Figgins's Antique

appears that among the matrices were six sets of Egyptians, 2-line great primer to brevier. In the specimen issued by Thorowgood in 1820, already mentioned, these Egyptians are displayed. But already, as early as 1815, in a specimen of Vincent Figgins there had appeared three sizes of Antique, upper case only, and in 1820 other founders had shown the letter, so that Thorne's priority is not beyond dispute. In the latter year, Edmund Fry's firm and Blake, Garnett & Co., of Sheffield, who had recently bought the foundry of William Caslon IV, both copied the design under the name of Antique. At least the probability is that Egyptian was the original name, and Antique the copy. In the following year, the original Caslon firm produced their version, also under the name Antique. In 1823, we find an Antique in the specimen of Wilson of Glasgow, while in 1825, Bower, Bacon & Co. ventured to use the original name, Egyptian. In an article in the *Archiv für Buchgewerbe* (Hft. 4, 1931), by Dr. H. Bockwitz, on Egyptians and grotesques, there will be found a list of some continental specimens which display the design, the earliest being that by Andreae of Frankfurt, of 1830.

Updike quotes a remark from a book of 1806 referring to the lettering of "fashionable Egyptian signboards". Whether this lettering had the characteristics of the founder's design does not appear. At least we can be confident that there was no Egyptian type in existence in 1806. Is it possible that the fat faces were originally so described? The bills of the lottery contractors are again a useful guide to the earliest appearance of the type; it was in regular use in the year 1817. There is one sheet referring to a draw to take place on January 21, 1817, which bears the imprint of one Thorowgood of Wood Street, Cheapside. This was a brother of William Thorowgood, and oddly enough, William is said to have purchased Thorne's foundry with the prize-money of a lottery ticket. From the Thorowgood sheet it follows that the type must have been on the market by 1816. William Hone was using the type in 1819, and in 1820 it is found frequently on sheets relating to the trial of Queen Caroline. From March 1821, it occurs on the play-bills of Drury Lane Theatre, and from that year onwards is not uncommonly used as a heading type in ordinary books.

The chief characteristics of Egyptian are the monotone, or almost monotone colour, and the horizontal square or slab serifs, which are almost equal in thickness to the main strokes. These characteristics, of course, result in a heavy black letter. The descenders, as one would expect in a type of the kind intended for display work, are very short. As the traditional Egyptians were designed by the men who had recently abandoned their old-face types in favour of the modern face, the new display type had naturally a number of features in common with the modern face. The upper case in particular had that monotonous uniformity of width which is found in all modern faces. Of individual letters, the G, the short-ranging J, and the R with a curved tail conform to the same standard. In the lower case, the e is the best example of the prevailing fashion. We have noted that the colour is not entirely monotone, and in this letter the stress is definitely vertical; the large eye of the e and the height of the t are further points. There have been other versions of the Egyptian under different names and various types derived from the same source. That freak type called *Italian*, and later *French Antique*, first displayed by the Caslons in 1821, seems to be inspired by the Egyptian. In this "monstrosity", to use Hansard's word, the serifs have become thicker than the main strokes; the design, so to speak, stands on its head. *Ionic* in some cases appears to be only another name for Egyptian.

SANS SERIFS

The third group of display types which was produced by the same generation of printers is that of the Sans Serifs. Although this group apparently did not come into use until the 1830's, it made, at any rate, one appearance in a specimen book of about 1816, that of William Caslon IV. In that book there is one line set in sans serif capitals, 2-line English in size. It seems then that the sans serifs also competed for the name Egyptian. The name was finally allocated to another style, and the type itself seems to have been an unsuccessful experiment on the part of Caslon, and we hear nothing more of it until 1832. In that year Vincent Figgins displayed it under the name sans serif and William Thorowgood, successor to Thorne, under the name grotesque. Thorowgood's specimen book of 1832 was a supplement and, as Figgins displayed more sizes of the type, it seems probable that he was the originator of this revival. In 1833 Blake and Stephenson of Sheffield showed the design as sans-surryphs, and in 1834 the Caslon firm followed with their version. Thorowgood's name, grotesque, seems hardly suitable, though not so absurd as the name gothic, given to it by the American and by some English founders. The name is presumably due to the fact that the early types in this style were heavy, black letters, which by their colour recalled the early gothic or blackletter types. Figgins's name at least describes one of the two main characteristics of the design, the absence of serifs. The other characteristic is the monotone colour, and equal weight of all strokes. The sans serif is in fact an Egyptian with the serifs knocked off, and it is probable that that was the manner of its creation.

The early sans-serif founts consisted of an upper case only, and all these capitals were of uniform width. Given the period in which it was first designed it was inevitable that, like the fat faces and Egyptians, the sans serifs should share that characteristic feature of the modern-face roman. This peculiarity in conjunction with the monotone face resulted in some of the letters being heavily over-weighted, for instance the G's and M's. The earliest founts were all of heavy weight, and it was some years before lighter faces were cut. The Caslon design, called Doric, was shown in a number of weights in their specimen book of 1857, but with no modification of the original forms. The addition of a lower case was of even later date, apparently not before the seventies in this country, although a German firm, Schelter & Giesecke, had displayed a lower case in 1850.

These three display types, the fat faces, the Egyptians, or Antiques, and the sans serifs, remained unchanged throughout the nineteenth century. The present-day revival of the three groups is an indication that there was something good in them. The manner in which they have been modified is in accordance with the change in our general typography; the letters have been made to conform to earlier and better designs, and the bad features derived from the modern-face roman have been eliminated.

As to the other display types of the nineteenth century, they certainly deserve Hansard's description of monstrosities. The ornamented three-dimensional letters such as appear in the Caslon specimen books of the mid-nineteenth century were doubtless cut in all seriousness, but are surely quite the worst letters ever shown in any founder's specimen.

CHAPTER NINE

Type Specimens

THE IMPORTANCE of type specimens for the study of typographical history is self-evident. In the pages of this book we have described several cases in which the discovery of hitherto unknown specimens has thrown a flood of light on the origin of particular designs. This source, of course, is almost entirely lacking for the early days of printing. Even when the type-founders were well established as a separate trade and had formed the habit of issuing sheets or books displaying their types, such specimens have often not survived down to our day. They were regarded as of temporary use and not as historical documents. It is only in comparatively recent years that attempts have been made to gather these documents together. In England the pioneers were William Blades and T. B. Reed. Charles Enschedé made a good beginning for the Dutch founders, whilst Gustav Mori, Friedrich Bauer and Marius Audin have collected much material relating to German and French founders.[1]

For the fifteenth century we have only one type specimen sheet, if we exclude the advertisement of Peter Schöffer of Mainz on which he gives a specimen of the Psalter type; the words "Hic est littera Psalteri" being set therein. Erhard Ratdolt's sheet, which like most of the earlier specimens, has survived in one copy only

[1] For a general list of Type Specimen Books and Sheets to 1800, see *The Library*, March 1942, pp. 1–20.

(at Munich), shows ten sizes of Rotunda, three of roman and one Greek. The sheet is dated April 1486, and was issued by Ratdolt on his return from Venice to his native city, Augsburg, no doubt for the convenience of possible customers for his press. He would not be selling type at that date to other printers. The next surviving sheet, also a unique copy (in the Börsenverein, Leipzig), is that of Johann Petri of Nuremberg, 1525, displaying three romans, two italics, a Greek, a Hebrew and two Frakturs. That these types or most of them were actually cut by Petri and were not merely his stock is inferred from what his brother-in-law, Johann Neudörffer, has to say of him in his *Nachrichten*. Neudörffer says that he was competent to make any instrument pertaining to printing. Petri again was a printer, and to what extent he was a founder working for other printers has not been worked out. At any rate Friedrich Pepyus of Nuremberg used some of his types. The next German type sheet, that of Valentin Geyssler, also of Nuremberg, 1561, was reproduced in *Ars Typographica*, vol. II, p. 232; this also is at Leipzig. Christopher Plantin's *Index Characterum* of 1567 is the first specimen book, and a very important one. It is again a printer's specimen, but from the documents preserved in the Antwerp Museum we can arrive at some conclusions concerning the men who cut his types. The specimens of Guillaume Le Bé reproduced by Henri Omont are really only proofs, not intended for publication, but the next sheet, that of the Egenolff-Berner Foundry, Frankfurt, 1592, is one of the landmarks in typographic history. It is not only the first undoubted specimen of a foundry, but has the further importance that the names of the designers of the types shown are appended to their designs. This sheet has already been referred to many times in these pages.

With the seventeenth-century specimen books begin to be more frequent. The Frankfurt house, however, continued to issue large broadsides and the other firms which set up in Frankfurt in competition followed their lead. Sheets issued by J. P. Fievet, Reinhard Voskens and his successor, J. A. Schmid, and in the next century J. H. Stubenvoll, C. A. Rolloux, J. F. Halle and J. H. Schippel, are known. Gustav Mori has published a book of reproductions of these Frankfurt sheets,[1] which are most helpful for the general history of types used in northern Europe. Many of the types displayed by the smaller Frankfurt firms were in fact the same as those of the Luther firm. These smaller men were often merely casters and not cutters of types.

Three early seventeenth-century books of type specimens are known. The first is that of G. L. Fuhrmann of Nuremberg, 1616 (copy in St. Brides Library). Here again by no means all the types shown, if any, were cut by Fuhrmann; some of the romans appear to be Garamond's and most of the italics Granjon's. For instance, we see the "Cicero currens" of the Egenolff sheet, 1592, which we have found to be in the stock of Plantin and also to be one of the Fell types. The second book is that of Jean Jannon of Sedan, 1622, the importance of which has already been considered; the third is the first specimen of the Stamperia Vaticana, Rome, 1628, a book fully described by Updike. After this book of 1628, there is a long gap in Italian specimens, apparently nothing more until we reach the generation of Bodoni. This century is, of course, the great age of the Dutch founders, chief of whom were Christoffel van Dijk and the Voskens. The Van Dijk specimen and the printer's specimens of the Elzeviers have been the subject of a special study by Charles Enschedé. Reproductions of other Dutch sheets of the period would be helpful, particularly in connection with English printing. We know that about 1700 there was much Dutch type in England. When does this Dutch importation begin and from what foundries? Probably not until after the Commonwealth.

In the eighteenth century there is no lack of material, especially in the Low Countries and France, in the generation of Fleischman and Rosart, of Luce and Fournier, and a little later of Bodoni in Italy. In this century in France the type specimen book reached its zenith; we have book after book of great beauty, while P. S. Fournier's *Modèles de Caractères*, 1742, is surely the most beautiful work of its class ever produced. Again we find a number of minor founders who apparently did not cut their own types, or only some

[1] *Frankfurter Schriftproben*, Frankfurt, 1955.

of them. It would be interesting to trace how many of Fournier's types are shown in the books issued by Louis Vernange, of Lyons, *c.* 1770, of J. L. Joannis, Paris, 1776, of H. Vaussy, Rouen, 1783, and of Perrenot of Avignon, 1784.[1] German eighteenth-century types are displayed in three books on printing in general, in Paulus Pater's *De Germaniae miraculo optimo, maximo, typis litterarum dissertatio*, 1710, in Ernesti's *Die woleingerichtete Buchruckerey*, 1723, and in C. F. Gessner's *Buchdruckerkunst und Schriftgiesserey*, 1740. These books are typical of the state of German printing at the time, and are all immeasurably below the French standard.

The series of specimens in England begins later than in other countries and at a low level. In one of the Humphry Dyson volumes of proclamations, made up in 1610, now in the Folger Shakespeare Library, Washington, there is bound in a specimen sheet bearing manuscript notes of an English printer. The sheet is set up partly in French, is very well printed, distinctly above the English standard of the day, while the notes give the prices of the types in "gulders". It would seem to be then a proof sent by a Netherlands founder, probably François Guyot, to his English customer and not to be an English specimen. The earliest known English specimen, that of an unknown English printer dating from about 1650, is preserved at the Oxford University Press. It bears no name, shows three sizes of roman and one italic, types all in common use in England, although of foreign origin. In the margins the sizes are written in in manuscript in the hand of Gerard Langbaine, who died in 1658. This specimen is reproduced in Berry and Johnson. It is typographically a poor affair, no better than the 1665 sheet of Nicholas Nicholls, preserved in the Record Office, or the copy of Moxon's specimen, 1669, in the British Museum. Of the other English founders of the seventeenth century we have nothing. However, in the Bagford and Ames collections in the British Museum, there are one or two unsigned sheets which probably were issued by the Andrews or

[1] For French specimens, see Audin, M., *Les Livrets typographiques des fonderies françaises*, Paris, 1933. Supplemented by Ellie Howe in *The Library*, June 1951.

Grovers. One, at any rate, is assigned to the Grovers in a note written by Joseph Ames. The Oxford Press specimens begin in 1693, but they of course display foreign types, with a few exceptions, as do the specimens of the two Edinburgh printers, James Moncur, 1710, and James Watson, 1713. The most valuable record we have of the earlier English founders is of much later date, namely, the Sale Catalogue of the James Foundry, 1782. Again only one copy has survived and unfortunately very little of each type is shown. Among these types are some of considerable antiquity which have already been referred to in this book; blacks, some probably of the sixteenth century, the great primer secretary used by Sir Walter Raleigh, the cursorials from the Grover foundry, and the Alexandrian Greek, a type dating from *c.* 1643 based on the earliest Greek Biblical manuscripts.

The first well-printed display of English types is the 1734 sheet of William Caslon. There are many copies known of this famous sheet bearing the date 1734, but only two of the real first edition, with the address Ironmonger Row, one in the British Museum and one in the library of the American Typefounders. The other editions, still dated 1734, but bearing the address Chiswell Street, appeared in Chambers's *Cyclopaedia* of 1738 and subsequent editions. Meanwhile Caslon himself had published other sheets, one in 1742, on which William Caslon II's name occurs for the first time, another in 1748 and a third in 1749. The increasing interest in the collecting of specimens is illustrated by the recent history of these sheets of 1742 and 1748. Reed, writing in 1887, referred to them as lost sheets. Updike sent a communication to *The Fleuron*, no. 1, describing a newly discovered copy of the 1748 sheet. It now appears that there is also a copy of this "lost" specimen in the Bodleian, and that of the 1742 sheet at least four copies are known. It was William Caslon who first began the practice of setting the text of his specimens in that notorious passage from Cicero's Catiline Orations which begins: "Quousque tandem. . . ." It is unfortunate that other English founders thought fit to copy him here, because the particular passage is ill chosen from the point of view of the number of letters occurring. There is, for example, no lower case g in the first few lines, so that g is never shown in the larger sizes.

In 1763 Caslon published his first specimen book, and from that date the Chiswell Street books have appeared at fairly regular intervals. In them we can trace the history of English typography in some detail. In 1785 we find William Caslon III's modern script, new developments of flowers copied from P. S. Fournier, and again of cast ornaments. Towards the end of the century we find the Baskerville imitations and in 1805 the earliest modern faces of the Caslon firm. A little later we meet the new advertising types, fat faces, Egyptians or Antiques, and finally sans serifs.

William Caslon was not the only type-cutter of his generation. Today John Baskerville's letter is rated at least as high. His specimen sheets, five in number, form an interesting and handsome group. The earliest, issued in 1754, is really a prospectus of his first book, the Virgil; the second of 1757 shows four sizes of his roman and italic, the third and fourth still more sizes, and the fifth, issued about the time of Baskerville's death in 1775, is a complete display of his work. Of this there is another issue bearing the date 1777, and further there are at least two French specimens of his types, published after the main part of his stock had been sold to Beaumarchais.

In the second half of the century the number of founders and specimens begins to increase, and many of them show the influence of Baskerville in their typography; for instance, those of Alexander Wilson, whose earliest specimen appeared in 1772, and the rare and attractive broadsides of Isaac Moore (Bristol, 1766, London, 1768 and 1770). Another contemporary, Thomas Cottrell, an old apprentice of Caslon, was the first founder to cast large poster letters, up to 12 lines pica, and the broadsides on which they are displayed are another rarity, only one copy of each, preserved at Stockholm, being known. To this generation belongs also the first specimens of an Irish founder, that of Stephen Parker of Dublin, 1769. The first two specimens of John Bell's British Letter Foundry, 1788 and 1789, are also known from a single copy only, in the Bibliothèque Nationale. Richard Austin, punch-cutter for John

Bell, afterwards had his own foundry in Worship Street, and the first specimen which he issued, in 1819, was unknown to Reed, who refers to a later edition of 1827. In the Victorian age the founders' specimens still have their value as documents in the history of typography, but have quite lost the attractive appearance of their predecessors in the eighteenth century.

LIST OF AUTHORITIES

THIS LIST is strictly confined to the subject of the book, namely the history of type designs. Books on the invention are not included, and only such histories of printing as have something of importance to say on typography. I have not included type specimens, although they are of course valuable sources for this study, except some which contain prefaces of importance. On the other hand, I have included the chief catalogues of type specimens. It is hoped that the list will be useful as a select bibliography of the subject.

AMES, JOSEPH. *Typographical Antiquities.* Edited by W. Herbert. T. Payne, London, 1785–90. 4to. 3 vol.

AUDIN, MARIUS. *Impressions de Louis Perrin.* M. Audin, Lyons, 1923. 4to. pp. 200–43.

— *Le Livre: son architecture, sa technique.* Lyons, 1924. 8vo. pp. xiii, 280.

— *Les Livrets typographiques des fonderies françaises,* Paris, 1933, 8vo. pp. xi, 193. Supplemented by Ellie Howe in *The Library,* June 1951.

AUSTIN, RICHARD. Specimen of Printing Types cast at Austin's Imperial Foundry. London, 1819. 8vo.
With an important preface by Austin on the subject of the modern face.

BASCHET, A. *Aldo Manuzio: Lettres et documents.* Paris, 1867. 8vo. pp. viii, 103.

BAUDRIER, H. *Bibliographie Lyonnaise. Recherches sur les imprimeurs, libraires, relieurs et fondeurs de lettres de Lyon au XVIe siècle.* Lyons, 1895–1921. 8vo. 12 vol.

BAUER, FRIEDRICH. *Chronik der Schriftgiessereien in Deutschland und den deutschsprächigen Nachbarländern.* Zweite Auflage. Offenbach a.M., 1928. 8vo. pp. xvi, 305.

The most complete account of German founders and their specimens.

BERNARD, AUGUSTE. *Geofroy Tory, peintre et graveur, premier imprimeur royal.* Deuxième édition. Paris, 1865. 8vo. pp. viii, 410.

— *L'Histoire de l'Imprimerie Royale du Louvre.* Paris, 1867. 8vo. pp. xii, 311.

BERRY, W. TURNER, and JOHNSON, A. F. *Catalogue of Specimens of Printing Types by English and Scottish Printers and Founders, 1650–1830.* Oxford University Press, 1934. 8vo.

Supplement in *Signature*, no. 16, 1952.

BIEDERMANN, L. W. VON. *Die deutsche Schriftgiesserei. Eine gewerbliche Bibliographie.* Bearbeitet von L. v. Biedermann. Herausgegeben von Oscar Jolles. Berlin, 1923. 8vo. pp. 271.

A valuable bibliography; deals with the history and technique of type-founding and ends with a list of German type specimen books.

BIGMORE, E. C., and WYMAN, C. W. H. *A Bibliography of Printing.* With illustrations. B. Quaritch, London, 1880–6. 4to. 3 vol.

Still the best bibliography of the subject. The notes are in many cases of considerable length and importance. Many of them were contributed by William Blades, the biographer of Caxton.

BIRRELL and GARNETT. *Catalogue of (I) Typefounders' Specimens; (II) Books printed in types of historic importance; (III) Works on Typefounding, Printing and Bibliography.* London, 1928. 4to. pp. vii, 105.

BODONI, G. B. *Manuale Tipografico*, Parma, 1818. 4to. 2 vol.
The preface contains Bodoni's remarks on type design. A translation of the preface by H. V. Marrot was published in London in 1925.

BRITISH MUSEUM. *Catalogue of books printed in the Fifteenth Century now in the British Museum.* London, 1908, etc. Fol.
Eight volumes have so far appeared, dealing with Germany, Italy and France.

— *A Guide to the Exhibition in the King's Library illustrating the History of Printing.* London, 1913. 8vo. pp. 100.

CARTER, H. "The Types of Christopher Plantin", *The Library*, September 1956.

CARTER, T. F. *The Invention of Printing in China and its spread westwards.* Revised edition. New York, 1931. 8vo. pp. xxvi, 282.
A shorter account of the Chinese invention appeared in *Ars Typographica*, vol. II, no. 1. July 1925.

CASLON, H. W. & CO. *Two Centuries of Type-Founding.* See McRae.

CHRISTIAN. A. *Débuts de l'Imprimerie en France.* L'Imprimerie Nationale. Paris, 1905. 4to. pp. xxiv, 343.
Each chapter is set in a different type, so that the book is also a specimen book of the Imprimerie Nationale. One chapter deals with Jaugeon and the "Romain du Roi".

CLAUDIN, A. *Histoire de l'Imprimerie en France au XVe siècle.* Paris, 1904–14. Fol. 4 tom.

COYECQUE, E. *Recueil d'actes notariés relatifs à l'histoire de Paris au XVIe siècle.* Paris, 1905, 1924. Fol. 2 vol.

— *Inventaire de la Collection Anisson sur l'histoire de l'imprimerie.* Bibliothèque Nationale, Paris, 1900. 8vo. 2 tom.

CROUS, E. *Die erste Probe Didotscher Lettern aus der Schriftgiesserei J. C. L. Prillwitz zu Jena.* Berlin, 1926. 4to. pp. 18.

— and KIRCHNER, J. *Die gotischen Schriftarten.* Leipzig, 1928. Fol. pp. 46, pl. 64.

DELISLE, L. *Recherches sur la librairie de Charles V.* Paris, 1907. 8vo. 2 pt.

DE VINNE, THEODORE. *Historic Printing Types: a lecture.* Grolier Club, New York, 1886. 4to. pp. 110.

— *The Practice of Typography.* New York, 1900–4. 8vo. 4 vol.

DIDOT, A. F. "Essai sur la typographie", extrait de *l'Encyclopédie moderne.* Paris, 1952. 8vo. pp. 558–922.

DIDOT, PIERRE. *L'Épître sur les progrès de l'imprimerie.* Paris, 1784. 8vo. pp. 20.

A poem. The notes are of considerable interest.

DIX, E. R. M. *The Earliest Printing in Dublin in the Irish, Latin, Greek . . . Languages.* Dublin, 1910. 8vo.

DREYFUS, J. *The Survival of Baskerville's Punches.* Cambridge, 1949. 8vo. pp. vii, 36.

DUERER, ALBRECHT. *Underweyssung der Messung, mit dem zirckel und richtscheyt, in Linien.* Mit zugehörigen figuren. Nuremberg, 1525. Fol.

A translation of the part relating to letters was published by the Grolier Club in 1917 under the title "Of the Just Shaping of Letters".

DUFF, E. GORDON. *Fifteenth-century English Books.* Bibliographical Society Monographs, no. 18, 1917. Fol. pp. ix, 36. pl. 53.

Shows all English types of the fifteenth century.

ENSCHEDÉ, CHARLES. "Die Druckerei der Elsevier und ihre Beziehung zu der Luterschen Schriftgiesserei." (*Die hochdeutschen Schriften von J. Enschedé en Zonen.* Haarlem, 1919.)

An English translation appeared in *Signature*, No. 10, 1938.

— *Fonderies de caractères et leur matériel dans les Pays-Bas du XVe au XIXe siècle.* Haarlem, 1908. Fol. pp. xxxiv, 404.

FAULMANN, C. *Illustrierte Geschichte der Buchdruckerkunst.* Vienna, 1881–2. 8vo. pp. viii, 806.

FOURNIER, P. S. *Manuel Typographique.* Paris, 1764–6. 12mo. 2 tom.

Tom. 1 is a technical account of type founding; tom. 2 is a type-specimen book, and includes an historical summary of all the foundries. An English version of tom. 1 by H. Carter was published in 1930.

FRITZ, GEORG. *Geschichte der Wiener Schriftgiessereien.* H. Berthold, Vienna, 1924. 4to. pp. 131.

FUMAGALLI, G. *Lexicon typographicum Italiae. Dictionnaire géographique de l'Italie pour servir à l'histoire de l'imprimerie dans ce pays.* Florence, 1905. 8vo. pp. xlvii, 587.

A mine of information on all branches of the printing trade in Italy.

GREY, N. *Nineteenth Century Ornamented Types.* London, 1938. 8vo. pp. 213.

HAEBLER, CONRAD. *Die italienischen Fragmente vom Leiden Christi das älteste Druckwerk Italiens.* Rosenthal, Munich, 1927. 4to. pp. 39. pl. 8.

— *Typenrepertorium der Wiegendrucke,* Berlin, 1905–24. 8vo. 6 pt.

HANSARD, T. C. *Typographia.* London, 1825. 8vo. pp. 924.

HART, HORACE. *Notes on a Century of Typography at the University Press, Oxford.* Oxford, 1900. Fol.

Shows all the "Fell" types and prints letters from Thomas Marshall as to purchases in Holland.

HESSEL, ALFRED. "Von der Schrift zum Druck", *Zeitschrift des Deutschen Vereins für Buchwesen,* 1923, pp. 89 *seq.*

Deals with the nomenclature of gothic hands.

ISAAC, F. *English and Scottish Printing Types, 1503–58*. Bibliographical Society, Facsimiles and Illustrations, nos. II and III. 1930–2. 4to. 2 vol.

A complete presentation of all types used in England and Scotland down to the end of Mary's reign.

— "Elizabethan Roman and Italic Types". *The Library*, June and September 1933.

A summary, with facsimiles, of types used in Elizabeth's reign.

JENKINSON, SIR C. H. *The Later Court Hands in England*. University Press, Cambridge, 1927. Fol. 2 pt.

— "English Current Writing", *Trans. of the Bibl. Soc.*, vol. XIII, 1915. pp. 273–95.

KAUTZSCH, R. *Die Entstehung der Frakturschrift*. Gutenberg Gesellschaft, Mainz, 1921. 8vo. p. 29. pl. 7.

KEYNES, SIR GEOFFREY L. *William Pickering, publisher: a memoir*. London, 1924. Fol. pp. 110.

LAPPENBERG, J. M. *Zur Geschichte der Buchdruckerkunst in Hamburg*. Hamburg, 1840. 4to. 2 pt.

LEGROS, L. A., and GRANT, J. C. *Typographical Printing Surfaces: the technology and mechanism of their production*. Longmans, London, 1916. 8vo. pp. xxiv, 732.

MCKERROW, R. B. *An Introduction to Bibliography for Literary Students*. Oxford, 1927. 8vo. pp. xv, 358.

Includes a chapter on Printing Types, and another on Elizabethan Handwriting.

MCMURTRIE, DOUGLAS. "A note on Script Types". *Ars Typographica*, vol. II, no. 2. 1925.

MCRAE, J. F. *Two centuries of Typefounding. Annals of the letter foundry established by William Caslon*. London, 1920. 4to. pp. xvi. 93.

MADAN, FALCONER, *A Chart of Oxford Printing*. Bibliographical Society Monographs No. XII. London, 1904. Fol. pp. 50.

MANZONI, GIACOMO. *Studii di bibliografia analitica.* Bologna, 1881, 1882. 8vo. 3 pt.

Concerned with Francesco Griffo, Vicentino and Tory, among others.

MARROT, H. V. William Bulmer—Thomas Bensley, *The Fleuron,* London, 1930. 4to. pp. 80.

Includes an account of the types of William Martin.

MAYER, ANTON. *Wiens Buchdrucker Geschichte, 1482–1882.* Vienna, 1883, 1887. 4to. 2 vol.

MORES, E. ROWE. *A Dissertation upon English Typographical Founders and Foundries.* London, 1778. 8vo. pp. 92.

One of the most important source books for the history of English types. Mores himself, at the time of the publication of his *Dissertation,* was the owner of the James Foundry, to which had descended the stock of several seventeenth-century founders. The work was reprinted by the Grolier Club, New York, in 1924.

MORI, GUSTAV. *Eine Frankfurter Schriftprobe vom Jahre* 1592. Frankfurt, 1920. Fol.

An account, with a reproduction, of an important specimen sheet, the earliest sheet of the Egenolff-Berner Foundry.

— *Frankfurter Schriftproben.* Frankfurt, 1955. Fol.

— *Die Schriftgiessereien in Süddeutschland und den angrenzenden Ländern.* Bauer, Stuttgart, 1924. 4to. pp. xx, 76. p. 19.

— *Schriftproben deutscher Schriftgiessereien und Buchdruckereien, 1479 bis 1840.* Ein Führer durch die Schrift-Proben-Austellung, Frankfurt, October 1926. Frankfurt, 1926. 8vo. pp. 54.

MORISON, STANLEY. *The Calligraphic Models of Ludovico degli Arrighi.* Officina Bodoni, Montagnola di Lugano, 1926. 8vo.

A reproduction of Vicentino's two writing books, with an account of his career as printer and type designer.

— Early Humanistic Script and the First Roman Type, *The Library,* June–September 1943. pp. 1–29.

MORISON, STANLEY. *The English Newspaper. Some account of the physical development of Journals printed in London between 1622 and the present day*. University Press, Cambridge, 1932. Fol. pp. xii, 335.

Apart from the subject of newspapers, the many reproductions in this volume are a valuable help for the study of English types.

— *The Fell Types*. (A Poster prepared for the Exhibition of Oxford University Press books held at Messrs. Bumpus's, November 1930. Not signed.)

— *Four Centuries of Fine Printing*. Upwards of six hundred examples, 1500–1914. Benn, London, 1924. Fol.

As a display of books printed in roman and italic, this is the best work we have.

— *German Incunabula in the British Museum*. Gollancz, London, 1928. Fol. pp. 26. pl. 152.

The introduction to this fine series of reproductions discusses the classification and nomenclature of gothic types.

— *Ichabod Dawks and his Newsletter*. Cambridge University Press, 1931. Fol. p. 38.

Concerned with the "Cursorials" of the Grover Foundry.

— *John Bell, 1745–1831, Bookseller, Printer, Typefounder, etc.* Cambridge University Press, 1930. 8vo. pp. xi, 165.

Reproduces all the specimen sheets of the British Letter-Foundry, whose types were cut by Richard Austin.

— "On Script Types", *The Fleuron*, no. 4, pp. 1–42. 1925.

The principal source for the study of the Latin scripts.

— "Towards an Ideal Italic", *The Fleuron*, no. 5, pp. 93–129. 1926.

Contains the first account of the John Bell types.

— "The Trusler Script Types", *The Fleuron*, no. 7, pp. 157–76. 1930.

MORISON, STANLEY. *Type Designs of the Past and Present, The Fleuron*, London, 1926. 8vo. pp. 70.

— "The Type of the Hypnerotomachia Poliphili", *Gutenberg Festschrift*, 1925. pp. 254–8.

The old-face romans are traced back to the Aldine roman cut by Francesco Griffo.

MOXON, JOSEPH. *Mechanick Exercises, or the Doctrine of Handiworks*, London, 1683. 4to. 2 vol.

Vol. II deals with printing and type-founding, the first work published in English dealing with the subject. In 1896 T. L. De Vinne published a reprint, and in 1901 the *Caxton Magazine* issued a facsimile reproduction of the second volume. A new edition, edited by H. Davis and H. Carter was published at Oxford in 1958.

— *Regulae Trium Ordinum Literarum Typographicarum, or the rules of the three orders of print letters, viz. the Roman, Italic and English.* London, 1676. pp. 51. pl. 38.

On the construction of letters with the rule and compass.

NEUDÖRFFER, J. *Nachrichten von Künstlern und Werkleuten des Nürnberger Schreibmeisters Neudörffer.* Herausgegeben von G. W. K. Lochner. Vienna, 1875. 8vo. pp. xxi, 237. Bd. X of *Quellenschriften fur Kunstgeschichte.*

OMONT, HENRI. *Spécimens de caractères Hébreux, grecs, Latins et de musique gravés a Venise et a Paris par Guillaume Le Bé, 1545–92.* Paris, 1889. 8vo. pp. 15.

The chief source of our information about Le Bé.

PICOT, E. *Note sur l'enlumineur parisien G. Richardière et sur son beau-père Ph. Danfrie.* Paris, 1889. 8vo. pp. 10.

On the civilité types of Danfrie.

PLANTIN, CHRISTOPHER. *Index Characterum.* Antwerp, 1567. 8vo.

The facsimile reprint published by D. C. McMurtrie, New York, 1924, includes some notes on the sources of the types displayed.

PROCTOR, R. *An Index to the Early Printed Books in the British Museum*. Part II, 1501–20. Section I. Germany. London, 1903. 8vo. pp. 273.

Contains reproductions of German types in use in the years 1501–20.

PYKE, R. L. *The Legibility of Print*. Stationery Office, London, 1926. 8vo. pp. 124.

REED, T. B. *A History of the Old English Letter Foundries*. London, 1887. 4to. pp. 380.

— A new edition, London, 1952. 4to. pp. xiv, 400.

RENOUARD, PH. *Imprimeurs Parisiens, libraires, fondeurs de caractères, à la fin du XVIe siècle*. Paris, 1898. 8vo. pp. xvi, 480.

A valuable work of reference, fully documented. A new edition has appeared serially in the *Revue des Bibliothèques*, 1925.

ROOSES, MAX. *Le Musée Plantin-Moretus*. Antwerp, 1913. Fol. pp. 407.

The fullest account of Plantin's press and his type-founders.

SABBE, M., and AUDIN, M. *Die Civilité-Schriften des Robert Granjon in Lyon, und die Flaemischen Drucker des 16. Jahrhunderts*. Vienna, 1929. 8vo. pp. 53.

SMITH, JOHN. *The Printers' Grammar*. T. Evans, London, 1787. 8vo. p. 369.

Includes a specimen of the Fry types, with a note on the relation of Fry to Caslon and Baskerville.

STATIONERY OFFICE. *Report of the Committee appointed to select the Best Faces of Type and Modes of Display for Government Printing*. London, 1922. 8vo. p. 18.

STOCKMEYER, I., and REBER, B. *Beiträge zur Basler Buchdruckergeschichte*. Basle, 1840. 4to, pp. viii, 158.

STOWER, C. *The Printer's Grammar; or, Introduction to the Art of Printing*. London, 1808. 8vo. pp. 562.

Includes specimens of the types of the principal London founders of the day.

STRAUS, R., and DENT, R. K. *John Baskerville, a memoir*. Chatto & Windus, London, 1907. 4to. pp. xi, 144.

THIBEAUDEAU, F. *La Lettre d'Imprimerie*. Paris, 1921. 8vo. 2 tom.

THE TIMES. *Printing in the Twentieth Century*. A survey. London, 1930. 4to. pp. xvi, 298.

TIMPERLEY. C. H. *Encyclopaedia of Literary and Typographical Anecdote*. London, 1830. 8vo. pp. 996.

TORY, GEOFROY. *Champ fleury*. Paris, 1529. Fol. 8vo.

Primarily a philological work, but includes much on the construction of letters. A translation by G. B. Ives was published by the Grolier Club in 1927, and a facsimile reproduction in Paris, 1931.

UPDIKE, D. B. *Printing Types, their history, forms and use*. Cambridge, Mass., 1922. 8vo. 2 vol. pp. 584.

— "A Translation of the Reports of Berlier & Sobry on Types of Gillé fils", edited by D. B. Updike, *The Fleuron*, no. 6, pp. 167–83. 1928.

A comment on the modern-face designs.

VOULLIÈME, E. *Die deutschen Drucker des fünfzehnten Jahrhunderts*. Berlin, 1922. Sm. Fol. pp. xvi, 175.

With many reproductions.

WARDE, MRS. B. (Paul Beaujon). "The Baskerville Types. A critique", *The Monotype Recorder*, September–October 1927.

— "The 'Garamond' Types. Sixteenth- and seventeenth-century sources considered", *The Fleuron*, no. 5, pp. 131–79. 1926.

— *The 1621 Specimen of Jean Jannon, Paris and Sedan, designer and engraver of the Caractères de l'Université*. Edited in facsimile. Chiswick Press, London, 1927. 8vo.

WARREN, ARTHUR. *The Charles Whittinghams, Printers*. Grolier Club, New York, 1896. 4to. pp. 344.

WATTENBACH, W. *Das Schriftwesen im Mittelalter, Dritte Auflage*. Leipzig, 1896. 8vo. pp. vi, 670.

WEGENER, J. *Die deutsche oberrheinische Type im 15. und 16. Jahrhundert.* 1904. 4to. p. 70.
Bd. 1 of the *Beiträge zur Bücherkunde.*

WILLEMS, ALPHONSE. *Les Elzevier. Histoire et annales typographiques.* Brussels, 1880, 1897. 8vo. 2 pt.

ZEDLER, G. *Von Coster zu Gutenberg. Der holländische Frühdruck und die Erfindung des Buchdrucks.* Leipzig, 1921. 4to. pp. viii, 194.

INDEX